APPLE

# Edible

Series Editor: Andrew F. Smith

EDIBLE is a revolutionary new series of books dedicated to food and drink that explores the rich history of cuisine. Each book reveals the global history and culture of one type of food or beverage.

## Already published

# Apple

## A Global History

*Erika Janik*

REAKTION BOOKS

*To my mom,*
*who liberally peanut-buttered*
*my apple slices as a child*

Published by Reaktion Books Ltd
33 Great Sutton Street
London EC1V 0DX, UK
www.reaktionbooks.co.uk

First published 2011

Printed and bound in China by C&C Offset Printing Co. Ltd

British Library Cataloguing in Publication Data

Janik, Erika.
Apple : a global history. – (Edible)
1. Apples – History.
2. Cooking (Apples).
3. Cider – History.
4. Cooking (Dates)
I. Title II. Series
641.34'11-DC22

ISBN 978 1 86189 848 7

# Contents

# Introduction

Although I grew up in Washington state, a place known for its apples, my first transcendent apple experience occurred 2,000 miles away in Wisconsin – a place more known for its cheese, sausage and beer than its apples. But there, at the Dane County Farmers Market in Madison, a homely, yellow-brown, faintly blushed Pink Pearl apple seduced its way into my bag and, later that night, turned my Red Delicious world upside down. The crisp skin gave way to a marbled pink and white interior so alternately sweet and tart on first bite that tears sprang to my eyes. How could an apple taste so good? And why had it taken more than two decades of good – but frankly, not great – apple consumption to reach this point?

The apple market had clearly changed since this hard-to-find Pink Pearl apple was developed in 1944, a descendant of an ancient line of red-fleshed Turkish crab apples. Although thousands of apple cultivars are known around the world, barely twenty varieties are widely available in local super-markets. Those twenty varieties account for 90 per cent of all apples consumed. Apples were one of the first fruits cultivated by humans and have long been one of the most important fruits in Europe, North America and other temperate regions of the globe – both for food and drink. But today apples

William Morris, 'Apple' wallpaper, 1877.

have become global commodities, valued more for their long storage life and transportability than for their astonishing variety and flavour.

The apple's story is, as Henry David Thoreau observed, remarkably 'connected with that of man'. Born in the mountains of Kazakhstan, it has travelled the globe and become, through its own prodigality and attachment to people, a species at home almost anywhere. The apple did such a convincing job of making itself at home in America that many Americans wrongly assume the fruit is a native.

Enmeshed in the folklore and history of nations around the globe, apples have been associated with love, beauty, luck, health, comfort, pleasure, wisdom, temptation, sensuality and fertility – and all this in addition to being just good eating and drinking. The apple has achieved its global prominence through its adaptability to local cultures and climates, its convenience and nutritional value, and its easy transport over long distances; all qualities that allowed the apple to infiltrate the world's soil and change how people ate in the process.

# I

# From Almaty to America

A seed hidden in the heart of an apple is an orchard invisible.
Welsh proverb

In early September of 1929, Nikolai Vavilov, famed Russian plant explorer and botanist, arrived in the central Asian cross-roads of Alma-Ata, Kazakhstan. Climbing up the Zailijskei Alatau slopes of the Tian Shan mountains separating Kazakh-stan from China, Vavilov found thickets of wild apples stretching in every direction, an extensive forest of fruit coloured russet red, creamy yellow and vibrant pink. Nowhere else in the world do apples grow thickly as a forest or with such incredible diversity. Amazed by what he saw, Vavilov wrote: 'I could see with my own eyes that I had stumbled upon the centre of origin for the apple.'

With extraordinary prescience and few facts, Vavilov suggested that the wild apples he had seen growing in the Tian Shan were in fact the ancestors of the modern apple. He tracked the whole process of domestication to the moun-tains near Alma-Ata, where the wild apples looked awfully similar to the apples found at the local grocery. Unfor-tunately, Vavilov's theory would remain mostly unknown for decades.

A branch thick with apples.

Auguste Renoir, *The Apple Seller*, c. 1890.

Exactly where the apple came from had long been a matter of contention and discussion among people who study plant origins. Vavilov, imprisoned by Joseph Stalin in 1940 for his work in genetics during the Lysenko Affair, died in a Leningrad prison in 1943. Only after the fall of communism in Russia did Vavilov's theory, made more than half a century earlier, become widely recognized.

As Vavilov predicted, it's now believed that all of the apples known today are direct descendents of the wild apples that evolved in Kazakhstan. Apples do not comprise all of Kazakhstan's plant bounty, however. At least 157 other plant species found in Kazakhstan are either direct descendants or close wild relatives of domesticated crops, including 90 per cent of all cultivated temperate fruits. The name of Kazakhstan's largest city, Alma-Ata, or Almaty as it is known today, even translates as 'Father of Apples' or, according to some, 'where the apples are'. So this news about the apple's origins was probably no surprise to residents, particularly in towns where apple seedlings are known to grow up through the cracks in the pavements. The apple has been evolving in Central Asia for upwards of 4.5 million years.

Plants producing apples belong to the genus *Malus*, which emerged about twelve million years ago in China and consist primarily of small trees and shrubs. A member of the flowering Rosaceae family, apples were among the first flowering plants on earth. The Rosaceae has given rise to many of the fruits that humans commonly eat, including pears, plums, peaches, strawberries and raspberries. Many of these fruits can also be found growing wild in the mountains of the Tian Shan, creating a veritable fruit forest.

Humans passing through the mountains of central Asia helped apples spread east and west. Travellers on the Silk Road, which passed through some of the richest apple forests, packed some of the biggest and tastiest fruits in their saddlebags to snack on as they made their journeys. Animals, too, helped the apple move overland. The apple's smooth, hard, teardrop-shaped seed has evolved to pass through an animal's digestive tract perfectly intact. An apple seed in the gut of a horse could be transported as far as 40 miles in a single day. As humans and animals travelled, seeds were dropped, seedlings grew and millions of unique apple types sprang up throughout Asia and Europe.

Creating apples of the same variety is not easy. Like humans, apples create offspring that differ, sometimes dramatically, from their parents. Every seed in an apple contains the genetic material for a completely new kind of apple. Each generation looks and tastes different. Were it not for grafting – the ancient technique of inserting the shoot or bud of one plant into the stem or trunk of another – every apple in the world would be its own distinct variety.

*Heterozygous* is the botanical term for this genetic variability. This, more than any other factor, accounts for the apple's ability to make itself at home in places as different from each other as Wisconsin, New Zealand, California, England, Chile and Kazakhstan. Wherever the apple tree travels, its offspring produce so many variations – several thousand per tree – that at least one is bound to have the qualities it needs to thrive in its new home.

Most of these novel trees produce bitter, unpalatable fruit, though these apples are still useful for making cider or feeding pigs. This is true in part because apple trees and apple eaters have different agendas. For an apple tree, it is more efficient to make many small apples than fewer big, fleshy apples. Many wild apples consist primarily of core, the part of the apple responsible for reproduction, with little of the edible flesh called the *torus*. Humans, on the other hand, want big apples with an enlarged torus for eating. The only way to guarantee these particular qualities is through grafting.

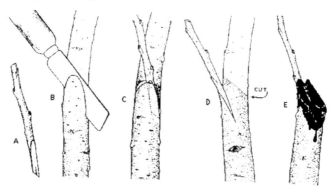

The five steps of grafting a tree, a way to propagate a particular variety of apple.

Much of the subsequent history of the domestic apple depends on the discovery of grafting. Before grafting, people marked out wild trees with good fruit and cut down those with bad-tasting fruits. We don't know who first discovered grafting but we do know that the Chinese and the Babylonians were both grafting plants more than 3,000 years ago. Each discovered that a slip of wood cut from a desirable tree or plant could be notched into the trunk of another tree or plant. The fruit produced from the wood that grew from that juncture would share the characteristics of its more desirable parent. Cato the Elder first described the grafting process in his *De Agricultura*, written in the second century BCE. This knowledge, along with the fresh fruit, travelled on the great long-distance trade networks that stretched from the eastern Mediterranean to the Indian subcontinent, so that by the first millennium BCE the cultivation and enjoyment of apples was considered essential to civilized life.

In Mesopotamia in the ninth century BCE, the Assyrian king's palace at Nineveh had orchards that grew 42 different kinds of fruit and gum trees. And in Anatolia, the Asian portion of modern Turkey, the Hittites, who flourished from 1600 to 1200 BCE, invested so heavily in fruit that penalties for the destruction of orchards and vineyards were written into their Law Codes.

Homer's *Odyssey*, written in the ninth or eighth century BCE, contains what many believe to be the first written mention of apples in the ancient world. When Mycenean hero Odysseus seeks refuge in the court of King Alcinous, he finds 'a large orchard of four acres, where trees hang their greenery on high, the pear and pomegranate, the apple with its glossy burden, the sweet fig and the luxuriant olive'. While this passage is commonly cited as the first mention of apples, the Greek word *melon* was used for almost any kind of round

Valley of the Hunza, Pakistan, where apricot, peach and apple trees grow.

fruit that grows on a tree. So the many legendary apples of Greek myth – the one given to Paris by Aphrodite, those thrown by Hippomenes to distract Atalanta or the apples growing in the Hesperides – may have been other kinds of tree fruit or perhaps no particular fruit at all. Later Greek writings drew a distinction between the apple and the quince, which had been growing in the region long before the apple. It's important to note, though, that Europeans interpreted these classical references to fruit as apples.

The rise of the Persian empire brought the enjoyment and celebration of fruit to a climax in the ancient world. At its height under Darius, around 512 BCE, the empire stretched from the Aegean coast of Turkey across Iran and Afghanistan to India, north to the edge of the Caucasus and into Central Asia, and south to the Middle East and around the Mediterranean coast to Egypt. Every royal and provincial palace had enclosed gardens of fruit trees and dining tables featuring the most exquisite fruits. These pre-Islamist Persians followed a dualist religion that aimed for harmony through the balance of opposites: apples, with their combination of sugar and acid, perfectly attained this harmony. Discerning Persian diners could distinguish between the different varieties and sources of apples: the best apples, the ones usually served at the Persian court, came from Georgia. Home-grown fruit, too, came to be an indication of a person's taste and the resources that he could invest in the selection and management of his orchards. Apples came to be associated with luxury, connoisseurship and social display for Persia's social elites, an association that drove gardeners to grow apples of ever-greater distinction for centuries afterwards.

When Alexander the Great conquered Persia in 334 BCE, he took many things from the Persians, including their appreciation of apples. This admiration soon spread throughout the Greek world. Alexander brought gardeners skilled in grafting from the Tigris basin to Greece to assist in the production of apples. Apples soon appeared on Greek tables, appearing in the final course of cakes and fruits served at grand banquets. Particular varieties of apples were highly sought after and the choicest apples carefully cultivated. In the first century CE, the Greek historian Plutarch called attention to the affection Greeks had for the apple:

> No other fruit unites the fine qualities of all fruits as does the apple. For one thing, its skin is so clean when you touch it that instead of staining the hands it perfumes them. Its taste sweet and it is extremely delightful both to smell and to look at. Thus by charming all our senses at once, it deserves the praise it receives.

The fruit, knowledge and dining customs of the Greeks and Persians moved west with the rise of the Roman Empire.

The Caves of Cappadocia. The frescoes of the 'Apple' church date mostly from the 11th century. The name is believed to have derived from the red fruit held by St Michael the Archangel in a fresco near the entrance.

Sir Edward Coley Burne-Jones and John Henry Dearle, *Pomona*, 1900, wool and silk tapestry. In Roman mythology, Pomona was the goddess of fruit trees and orchards. Here Pomona cradles several apples in her gathered skirts.

POMONA

Unique fruits and improved horticultural skills were eagerly brought back to Rome along the Silk Road trade routes connecting Rome to China. Among the fruits introduced to Rome were sweet cherries, peaches, apricots and oranges. Italy became one vast orchard, so much so that the fruit trees even had their own deity, the goddess Pomona.

Bust of Athena rising from the ground grasping an apple in her left hand, attributed to the Bowdoin Painter, 480–440 BCE.

Orchards, vineyards and olive groves offered wealthy Romans a quiet refuge from frenetic city life. Gardens provided their owners a little piece of paradise and no garden was complete without apple trees. The Romans had more varieties of apples in cultivation than any other fruit and considered the apple a luxury item. According to Pliny the Elder, the Romans cultivated 23 different varieties of apples. Presenting someone with apples you had grown yourself was considered a high compliment in Rome, as it had been in Persia. In turn, these estate owners produced a large body of work offering advice and instruction on everything from grafting and harvesting, to storage and pest control.

Fruit gardening both encouraged and was encouraged by the custom of outdoor dining. Romans created dining rooms under the sky where diners ate among the fruit trees. According to the Roman poet Horace, the perfect Roman meal began with eggs and ended with fruit, giving rise to the proverbial Latin expression *ova ad malum*, 'from the egg to the apple', the equivalent of today's English idiom 'from soup to nuts'.

The Romans almost certainly spread the domestic apple from Europe across the English Channel to Britain. Before the Romans arrived, the inhabitants of Europe and Britain had made good use of their native crab apples, mostly for drinking. These native crab apples were not, however, to the taste of the incoming Romans, who preferred the comforts of home and its perfect, sweet fruits. So they established orchards in Spain, France and Britain that were planted with their favourite apples from home. The tiny Lady apple, which often shows up around Christmastime in Europe, is thought to be one of them. A Roman mosaic at St-Romain-en-Gal in south-eastern France depicts the progress of an apple from grafting through to harvest.

The cultivation and enjoyment of apples, as well as other fresh fruit, remained widespread throughout the duration of the Roman empire. Towards the end of the fourth century, when the empire began to collapse, however, much of the fruit-growing went with it. Roman orchards in Britain did not often survive the withdrawal of the legions and the influx of Jutes, Angles and Saxons from northern Germany. In France,

Jacobus de Cessolis, *Liber de Scacchis*, a 13th-century book. Here the apple is symbolic of royalty: the king is holding 'an apple of gold', or orb.

the invading Franks showed concern for the orchards but not so much for the finer points of cultivating the highest quality apples. As a result, many varieties and horticultural skills went into decline and could have been lost altogether had it not been for the orcharding traditions of the Christian and Islamic faiths.

With their practical as well as ideological commitment to self-sufficiency, monasteries became repositories of collected cultural and intellectual skills after Rome was overrun. Monastic orders had long been committed to feeding themselves by growing gardens filled with edible plants and fruits. By growing everything within the monastery walls, the monks would never need to go outside. Apples, therefore, followed the abbeys.

Monastic skills and fruit-growing were further encouraged with the crowning of Charlemagne as Holy Roman Emperor in 800 CE. Charlemagne's ninth-century *Capitulare de Villis* (Rules of Land Use) decreed that royal lands in every city should be planted with apples, cherries, plums, peaches and pears. Among the varieties of apples listed were perfumed apples, sweet apples, sour apples and early- and late-keeping apples. Charlemagne also encouraged brewers, which included cider-makers, to develop their trade.

Continued Danish and Viking invasions in Britain left apples a low priority on the island until the Norman Conquest in 1066. The Norman invasion changed the legal and social structure of England and brought the island into closer contact with the European mainland. More importantly, however, the Normans brought their enthusiasm for fine cider.

In twelfth-century Europe, the expansion of the Cistercian order of monks, a breakaway group of Benedictines, renewed the cultivation of apples across the continent. The Cistercian monks valued manual labour and the cultivation of abbey lands, and they worked hard to propagate and distribute good varieties of fruit. As Cistercian abbeys spread to Scotland, Germany, Sweden, Portugal and the eastern Mediterranean, orchards went with them. Successful grafts from one orchard were shared with other Cistercian monks around Europe. The effect of all this Cistercian orcharding was to encourage monastic fruit-growing in general.

As Western Europe struggled with invaders after the fall of Rome, the Byzantine Empire in Eastern Europe continued to flourish until the seventh and eighth centuries, when it, too, was overrun. The invaders this time were the newly emergent followers of Islam, but unlike those in the West, these conquerors had received strict orders to preserve crops and orchards. With the restoration of peace, the horticultural

Ali Muhammed Isfahani, ceramic tile, 1884–5. Young men read poetry accompanied by male and female attendants in an orchard in this Iranian tile.

skills of Byzantium and Persia became part of Islamic life. The Muslim world encouraged scholarship, gardening and fruit-growing. Muslims translated and updated botanical works from Greece and Rome. New kinds of fruit and new varieties were introduced and acclimatized. Moorish Spain, in particular, became a centre of horticultural expertise and the sultan established sophisticated gardens at Toledo and Seville. Among the crops acclimatized to the Iberian Peninsula by the tenth century were rice, sorghum, sugar cane, cotton, oranges, lemons, limes, bananas, pomegranates, watermelons, spinach, artichokes and aubergines (eggplants). Islam not only preserved the fruit-growing wisdom of the classical world, but expanded and improved it.

By the thirteenth century, apples were again grown with increasing frequency throughout Europe. The number of named apple varieties soared as cultivating the best and most beautiful apples became a mark of wealth and culture, as it had been in Rome and Persia before. Apples became an essential part of daily life, so much so that explorers and colonists could not bear to leave home without a favourite variety. Seeds from these apples travelled to almost every corner of the globe.

The colonists who left Europe in growing numbers throughout the sixteenth and seventeenth centuries planted apples all along the eastern seaboard of North America. Some of the earliest colonists tried growing some of their grafted Old World apple trees, but most did not fare well in their new environment. These colonists also planted seeds and took them west to establish orchards in the Midwest, and on the Pacific coast by the late nineteenth century.

Apples also proliferated in South America, planted by Spanish and Portuguese explorers and colonists. Apples became so common and vigorous that by the time Charles Darwin landed in Chile in 1835, he found apple trees growing all along the coast, virtually obscuring the Chilean port of Valdivia.

Dutchman Jan van Riebeeck, founder of the Netherlands East India Company trading post at Cape Town, took apples to South Africa in 1654. He made fruit-growing a requirement among settlers so they could both feed themselves and supply trading boats heading east. Apples remained a minor agricultural industry until the late nineteenth century, when an infestation of the root louse known as *phylloxera* destroyed the Cape's grape vineyards. Cecil Rhodes, founder of the British state of South Africa, turned to apples as an alternative. Rhodes purchased several farms in the 1890s, many of them bankrupt vineyards, and combined them under the name Rhodes Fruit Farms to prove that fruit could grow well

Russell Lee, *Orchards in Hood River Valley*, 1941. Orchards cover the Hood River Valley of Oregon, with Mount Hood in the background.

and profitably in South Africa. Working closely with California fruit-growers, Rhodes helped to build the fruit industry that flourishes there today.

Australia got its first apples when Captain Arthur Phillip established the English settlement of Port Jackson (today's Sydney) in 1788. How many of these apples survived that original planting is not known. That same year, the infamous Captain Bligh anchored his ship, the *Bounty*, off the coast of Tasmania. The ship's botanist planted three apple seedlings and several apple and pear seeds, laying the foundations for the island's later moniker as the 'Apple Isle'. As settlement in Australia and New Zealand took off, so too did its orchards, so much so that the fruit-growing area around Hawkes Bay, New Zealand, became known as the 'Apple Bowl'. The seasonal opposition of the southern and northern hemispheres helped the apple industries in Australia and New Zealand to boom, allowing them to supply fruit to apple-loving Americans, Canadians and Europeans in the winter months.

Over thousands of years, apples have followed the west-ward course of empire, travelling from Central Asia to the ancient world to Europe, and then on to the Americas with the explorers and colonists. In an essay written in praise of wild apples in 1862, Henry David Thoreau wrote that the apple 'emulates man's independence and enterprise. It is not simply carried . . . but, like him, to some extent, it has migrated to this New World, and is even, here and there, making its way amid the aboriginal trees.' Along the way, the apple has accu-mulated a vast store of genes that has allowed it to thrive nearly everywhere in the temperate world.

# 2
# Food of Legend

Stay me with flagons, comfort me with apples,
for I am sick of love.
Song of Solomon 2:5

As apple trees took root around the world, its fruit took root
in art, poetry, music, mythology, legend and prose almost
immediately. The apple inspired an explosion of literature
and illustration, a degree of adulation nearly impossible to
imagine for any other fruit.

At some time, apples have symbolized nearly every kind
of fruit. Whenever a new fruit or vegetable was discovered
that was round and sized somewhere between a cherry and
a pumpkin, it was often called an 'apple' until given a name
of its own. The list of foods called 'apple' at some point
includes everything from avocados and cashews to aubergines (eggplants) and pine nuts – not to mention baseballs
in nineteenth-century America. Humans just could not help
but see apples everywhere.

Apples also played a starring role in many stories and
legends. Apples are commonly believed to be the fateful fruit
in the Garden of Eden; Aphrodite often carried an apple in
her hands, as did the Scandinavian goddess Idun; an apple

Charles Holroyd,
*Eve and the
Serpent*, 1899.
In this print
Eve leans
against a tree
in the Garden
of Eden while
picking an apple.

precipitated the Fall of Troy; the Druids selected divining rods from apple trees; Muhammad inhaled eternal life through an apple brought to him by an angel; and Snow White received a poisoned apple from the evil queen. The apple's remarkable biological adaptability gave the fruit a cultural relevance in

'The Apple Tree in
the Garden of Eden',
1577, woodcut.

places as different as Turkey and Norway, and led to the creation of a vast collection of imagery, symbolism and stories attached to the apple. Yet for all the diversity of places and cultures in which apples appeared throughout the centuries, the apple called to mind remarkably similar themes and ideas of paradise, love, magic, fertility and immortality.

Of all the ideas associated with apples, the notion of paradise most immediately springs to mind. Most modern Christians suppose that Eve snatched the apple for Adam at the serpent's bidding, forever banishing them from Paradise. But the original Hebrew text says only 'fruit', never specifying which fruit, apple or otherwise. However, artistic depictions of the event, ranging from serious religious paintings to cartoons, invariably show an apple as the fruit in question.

The apple began appearing in devotional pictures, often mythical depictions of the Garden of Eden, in Western art in the Middle Ages. Early Christian scholars often took the forbidden fruit to be an apple, possibly because the Latin word *malum* means both 'apple' and 'evil'. It also probably helped that apples were more popular in Europe, where most of these Christians lived, than in the Middle East.

The idea of sweet apples growing in the Garden of Eden, on land between the Tigris and Euphrates rivers, is improbable. Apple seeds require a cold chill to germinate, a climactic condition that did not exist in Mesopotamia, today's Iraq. The Eastern Church, perhaps more sensibly given the climate, favoured figs as the forbidden fruit. The struggle between apples and figs as the dominant symbol of temptation played out for centuries in Christian iconography. Physically, the apple had a lot going for it as the fruit of temptation: a red (symbolizing blood) or golden (symbolizing greed) colour; a

A folio from a prayer book depicting Adam and Eve, *c.* 1300–25.

round (symbolizing fertility) shape; and a sweet (symbolizing desire) taste. But working in the fig's favour, besides the climate, is what happened after Adam and Eve ate the forbidden fruit: they covered themselves with leaves usually said to be from a fig tree. Just to confuse matters more, some modern scholars now believe the fruit to have been a pomegranate. Islamic

Albrecht Dürer, *Adam and Eve*, 1504. In this engraving Eve takes the fruit offered to her by the serpent as Adam reaches out to take it.

tradition still commonly represents the forbidden fruit as a fig or olive. No matter the intended fruit, after the Garden of Eden the possession of apples came to be associated with desire, fecundity, danger and the reward of immortality.

Christians weren't the first to pick up on the apple's racy side. One of the most well-known Greek myths concerns the golden apple labelled 'To the fairest' that Eris, goddess of strife and discord, threw among the guests at the wedding celebration of Peleus and Thetis. The apple caused a quarrel among Hera, Aphrodite and Athena, with each claiming the apple, and its inscription, for herself. They eventually agreed to make Paris, the son of the King of Troy, settle the dispute. After much bribery among the goddesses, Paris chose Aphrodite, who had promised him the hand of the most beautiful woman in the world, Helen of Sparta, in return. This promise ultimately resulted in the Trojan War. The moral of the story: apples may look enticing, but they can be trouble. Christian scholars knew these Greek myths and probably adapted many of the ideas and themes associated with them to their new religion.

The Trojan War wasn't the only time Aphrodite became involved with apples. Aphrodite, the Greek goddess of love, and her Roman counterpart Venus, revered apples, and depictions of her frequently featured apples. As a result, apples appear in many Greek myths involving love, courtship and marriage, perhaps most famously in the story of Atalanta. Racing all of her suitors to avoid marriage, Atalanta manages to outrun all but Hippomenes, who defeated her not by speed, but by cunning. Using three golden apples given to him by Aphrodite, Hippomenes threw them at Atalanta, distracting her enough to win the race and Atalanta's hand in marriage as the prize. Hurling apples at another person was a common practice in ancient Greece, signalling romantic interest among

John Simon (1690–1751), *Judgment of Paris*, mezzotint. Paris is handing the apple to Venus (the Roman name for Aphrodite), the precipitating act of the Trojan War.

single men and women. Additionally, success or failure in love could be foretold by spitting apple seeds at the ceiling.

In Armenian folk traditions, apples also played a part in courtship, often signalling that some desire, usually love, had

Roman marble statue of Aphrodite holding an apple, 2nd century CE.

Luke Clennell, *Hippomenes and Atalanta*, 1811. Hippomenes is tossing an apple toward Atalanta in the distance.

HIPPOMENES AND ATALANTA,
*Frontispiece Vol 37.*

been attained. Many tales end with the phrase 'Three apples fell from heaven', the equivalent of the familiar 'And they all lived happily ever after'. While there are a few instances of the phrase in other countries, it appears to be a distinct Armenian tradition, with the only variation being the source of the apples: sometimes God rather than heaven drops the fruit. Within the stories, apples often signal love and immortality, as well as the simple gift of friendship.

Along with love and desire, apples could also foretell fertility. Throughout European, Asian and North American folklore, apples serve as predictors of love and childbearing. The association is scarcely surprising given the apple's related ties to love and desire. Greek dramatists, including Aristophanes and Theocritus, wrote comic punch lines on the resemblance between apples and a woman's breast, a visual refrain that recurs throughout the entire sweep of Western art.

Apple-related fertility stories and practices span the continents. In the thirteenth-century Icelandic Volsunga Saga (the Germanic version of which forms the root of Wagner's *Ring* cycle), a goddess dropped an apple into the lap of a childless king who prayed for a son. A son was soon born and that son kept an apple tree in his centre hall to symbolize the continuance of his family. Traditional Kyrgystani women who are unable to conceive will roll on the grass beneath an apple tree to make themselves fertile. Montenegrin brides will throw an apple on the roof of their new husbands' house to encourage the birth of many children. Women posed beneath fruit trees or bearing fruit have been favourite motifs in Indian and Chinese art for centuries, symbolizing fecundity, prosperity and plenitude. Apples also symbolized peace in China and were considered especially good luck if they happened to be red. In Belgium, Walloon women test their mating fates with apple seeds. Seeds are placed on the lid of a hot pan and a woman asks, 'Will I like him?' If the answer is yes, the seeds will explode. The game continues through a succession of questions —'Will he marry me?' 'Will we have children?' 'Will my first child be a boy?' – and each time the seeds burst, the answer is yes. The answer to the final question, how many children will she have, corresponds to the total number of seeds that have burst.

Apple seeds account for much of the superstition so long attributed to apples. Cut an apple in half vertically into two equal halves and you'll see some resemblance to the female

'Young Man under apple trees; Good Seed brings good fruit', 1486, woodcut.

genital system. Slice an apple at its equator and you'll find five small chambers, each with a seed inside, arrayed in a symmetrical starburst shape like a pentagram, one of the most widely used religious symbols in the world. The pentagram was also a key to the occult sciences, said to reveal the secret knowledge of good and evil. Magicians used the pentagram for casting spells or enchantments, such as the spell cast on the apple given to Snow White. The magician Merlin also sat beneath an apple tree to teach, and apples were eaten in Brittany before prophecies were made.

The connection between the seeds of plants and fertility was so strong that the words for seed and semen remained the same in French and other Romance languages into the nineteenth century. Therefore, many people believed that identifying and surrounding yourself and your family with seeds was roughly analogous to making an offering to the gods and goddesses of fertility, which would, hopefully, guarantee your family's perpetuity. Although nearly all fruits, grains and flowers have at one time or another served as talismans of fertility, none have had the longevity and geographical range of the apple.

Frequently associated with the colour gold or yellow, apples also took on the power of that colour, which was thought to confer immortality. The idea of access to immortality gained from magical fruit permeates myths from the Middle East to Scandinavia, and the further north the culture, the more often the immortal fruit in question is an apple. One common feature of these stories is the rarity of immortality and the difficulty of attaining it. Among the Greeks, the golden apples of immortality grew on a tree hidden in an orchard near Atlas. The nymph daughters of Atlas, the Hesperides, protected the apples, with the help of a dragon, from giants who continuously tried to steal them. Hercules later stole these apples as one of his twelve labours. Simply possessing the apples guaranteed immortality, a right the gods reserved for themselves.

More than a thousand miles north, a similar story recounts a struggle between giants and the Nordic gods in Asgard. Idun, the goddess of spring and rebirth, was the keeper of the golden apples, to which the gods owed their continuous youth and immortality. Giants and other mortals endlessly schemed to capture Idun so they could steal immortality for themselves. One of the more clever giants, the storm giant Thiassi, once managed to abduct Idun and her apples. As soon as Idun left Asgard, the gods began to age rapidly. They discovered that Loki, the trickster god, was the last one seen with Idun and demanded that he rescue her or become the first immortal to die. Loki flew to the giant's home disguised as a falcon. He changed Idun into a nut and carried her away to safety in his claws. The gods were restored to youth soon after.

Gilded bronze statue of Hercules from the 2nd century BCE, possibly the cult statue from the Temple of Hercules Victor that stood by the ancient cattle market in the Forum Boarium. He holds his club in his right hand and the three apples of the Hesperides in his left.

While not quite guaranteeing immortality, apples were also said to at least make you live longer, a power that greatly interested the Macedonian king Alexander the Great. On the same expedition in which he sought the Water of Life in central Asia, Alexander allegedly found apples capable of prolonging the lives of the priests who ate them by as much as 400 years. Alexander apparently did not eat enough of these apples himself, as he died at the age of 33.

Along with immortality, strains of mysticism run through Celtic myths and legends concerning apples. Numerous Celtic stories find heroes sleeping beneath apple trees only to be carried off by otherworldly women. In other stories, apples confer everlasting youth or provide magical sustenance. In one Celtic legend, the White Goddess summons the god Bran to the Land of Youth, one of the most popular Celtic otherworlds, with a 'silver white-blossomed apple branch' from Emain Ablach, an island where the apple trees were said to bloom and fruit at the same time. Gods and goddesses from the Land of Youth usually carried an apple branch bearing golden fruit with tinkling leaves so musical that mortals would be lulled to sleep on hearing it. Another story finds the Irish hero Oisín in the Land of Youth, where he sees himself mounted on a white horse pursuing a beautiful woman on horseback holding a golden apple. And when Conle, another Irish hero, is given an apple by a beautiful fairy woman, it nourishes him for a month and eventually leads him to go away with her in a crystal boat; he is never again seen among the living.

The Celtic myths and legends had nothing on Sir Thomas Malory's fifteenth-century story of Camelot and King Arthur, however. This legendary figure who, according to medieval histories, folklore and literary invention, led the defence of Britain against Saxon invaders, developed as a figure of international interest largely through the popularity of Geoffrey of Monmouth's imaginative twelfth-century *History of the Kings of Britain*. Malory's version blended French and Celtic lore through the lens of the Christian Crusades and the search for the Holy Grail. The search for the Grail eventually captured all of Arthur's trusted friends and officers until only Arthur was left to fight his traitorous son Mordred at the battle of Camlann. Mordred is killed and Arthur fatally wounded in battle. Arthur is then taken to Avalon, a magic island where the golden apples of immortality grew.

The name Avalon comes from the Celtic prefix *av* or *af*, which means apple. In fact, all European languages other than the Romance languages use a word with a root *ap, ab, af* or *av* for apples and apple trees: the German *apfel*, for example, Irish *abhal*, Icelandic *epli* and Welsh *afal*. Many British place names contain the apple prefix, including Avening, Avington, Avon and Aviemore. Other names are more obviously apple-related, such as Apperknowle in Derbyshire, Appleby Castle in Cumbria, Appledore in Devon, Appledram and Applesham in Sussex, and Appletreewick in Yorkshire. At least 47 British places include a reference to apples in their names, a clear indication of the fruit's importance to the Celts and later the Anglo-Saxons.

Geoffrey had first described Avalon in *The Life of Merlin*. According to Geoffrey's account, on Avalon crops grow untended, 'apple trees spring up from the short grass of its woods' and men live for a hundred years or more. Scholars have sought to identify the location of Avalon for centuries. Some have identified Avalon as Glastonbury, a town not far from Stonehenge that has had mystical and spiritual overtones since before the Romans arrived.

Apples played a heroic role for the Swiss in the legend of William Tell. Tell, a peasant from Burglen in the Swiss canton

Heinrich Petri, *Wilhelm Tell*, 1552, woodcut. Wilhelm Tell takes aim at the apple on his son's head.

of Uri in the thirteenth and early fourteenth centuries, defied Austrian authority by refusing to swear allegiance to the Habsburg crown. Seized by the bailiff Hermann Gessler, Tell was ordered to shoot an apple off his son's head with his crossbow. Placing one arrow in his crossbow and taking aim, Tell managed to shoot the apple clean off his son's head. Tell's bravery in the face of Gessler's repeated treachery inspired the Swiss to throw off the yoke of Austrian oppression and to pledge to live forever free.

While a fantastic story, there is no evidence for the existence of William Tell. The central idea of the story – a marksman forced to shoot an object from the head of a loved one – first appeared in Norse sagas written centuries before the fifteenth-century Swiss version. The Tell legend attained world renown through German dramatist Friedrich von Schiller's 1804 play *Wilhelm Tell*, which was based in part on ancient Swiss chronicles. Fictional or not, the idea of a deeply moral and fervently nationalistic Tell expertly shooting an apple hardened the resolve of the Swiss to resist domination throughout the succeeding centuries.

Not satisfied with apple tales, legends and symbols, many people in the Middle Ages began searching for the Garden of Eden and its infamous apple tree. They believed that the garden had not been destroyed but had survived the Flood and could be found on some remote hilltop somewhere in the world. Once explorers started roaming the globe, the idea floundered, replaced by the notion that after the Fall the contents of Eden had been scattered to the corners of the globe. Every newly discovered plant and animal, therefore, represented a piece of the Garden's puzzle, which would one day be reassembled. Botanical gardens, which grew in popularity in Europe in the sixteenth century, became a way of piecing together Eden and recovering lost knowledge. Many thought gardens could also help them regain Adam's power over nature, which he lost during the Fall, raising the prospect that, like Adam's garden, these gardens might transcend climate and season. As a result, an immense amount of energy was expended in collecting, cataloguing and exchanging plants.

Botanical gardens emerged in the Middle East and Central Asia much earlier than in Europe because of Islam, a religion strongly associated with gardening. In Islam, gardens served as the earthbound analogues for the life in Paradise promised to believers in the Qu'ran. Gardening had a high value and enclosed garden spaces became central to Islamic cities and homes. In fact, the Prophet Muhammad's own home garden in Medina became the first place of Islamic worship. Many of the Islamic empire-builders that spread across the Mediterranean and Asia after 600 CE became garden-makers as well.

The rise of Protestantism in the sixteenth century only helped to cement the apple's place in Western religious iconography. Countries that became predominantly Protestant saw the apple as the fruit not only of God but of country too, as national identities became linked to religious beliefs. In anticipation of the second coming of Christ, Protestants sought to repair the corruption of nature that had occurred after the Fall when Adam and Eve were expelled from the Garden of Eden. Like the creation of botanical gardens, the planting and tending of orchards was high on the list of improving activities.

Walter F. Osborne, *Apple Gathering, Quimperle*, 1883.

Everywhere that Protestantism went, orcharding followed. Apples appealed to Protestant sensibilities more than any other fruit. The trees were thought neither greedy nor temperamental, and rewarded the diligence of the planter with good, useful and long-lasting food – all qualities that Protestants admired and tried to cultivate in themselves. English Protestants even wrote books on the divine meaning of orchards, such as *The Spiritual Use of an Orchard* by English Calvinist Ralph Austen. Moreover, one Christian tradition held that the real damage in the Garden of Eden happened when God made Eve from Adam's rib. These Protestants embraced the apple as spiritually superior because they mistakenly believed that the trees created fruit asexually, a living monument to the ideal of undivided nature found in Paradise and in Adam before Eve (the apple tree, in fact, like many other fruit trees, will not bear unless it has been fertilized with the pollen of another variety by birds or insects). When the Catholic backlash sent Protestants fleeing to Holland, England and North America, they took their apples and apple stories with them.

Apples became the first fruit of America. Many colonists felt that settling in the New World held the prospect of universal redemption, a second chance for humans. Planting an apple orchard was an essential part of that vision of a new Jerusalem, nearly as important as putting a roof over one's head. Claiming land with apple orchards symbolized the achievement of the colonists, visible proof of their mastery over the primordial wilderness. Planting apple seeds also had a practical purpose. They encouraged settlers to put down roots, since apple trees could take as long as ten years to fruit. Settlers in the American Midwest had no choice but to plant orchards, as grants of land specifically required the planting of 'at least fifty apple or pear trees'.

Some thought that the New World contained the seeds of the actual Paradise; they needed only to be released and planted in the continent's fertile, redemptive soil to spring forth once again. And no one claimed more of that land and released more seeds than the legendary Johnny Appleseed.

Born John Chapman in Massachusetts in 1774, Johnny Appleseed wandered through the wildernesses of Pennsylvania, Ohio, Illinois and Indiana planting apple seeds and becoming a folk hero in the process. He was a follower of the Swedish mystic Emanuel Swedenborg, who believed that every plant, animal and object in nature corresponded with particular spiritual truths. Chapman's wanderings found him well placed to propagate trees and proselytize Swedenborg's faith.

Chapman, like many other nineteenth-century utopians and transcendentalists, saw God in nature and believed that an understanding of the natural world went hand-in-hand with spiritual knowledge. For Chapman, man was critical to the expansion of the American prospect; he must not just observe nature, but engage and develop it to recover the limitless natural diversity of the original Garden of Eden. He also believed that if America were filled with apple trees, then no man, woman nor child would ever go hungry again.

Chapman planted only seeds, no grafts, because he wanted to reveal the vast multiplicity of apple types contained within each apple. Hundreds of new apples never seen anywhere in the world grew across the American frontier. One of his favourite varieties was the Rambo apple, which originated in Sweden and, strangely enough, inspired David Morrell to name his action hero Rambo, made famous on film by Sylvester Stallone. The apples planted by Chapman were richer in diversity than anything Americans and Europeans had yet known, a utopian prospect no longer imaginable on the overpopulated farms of Europe. As he travelled westward into Indiana, he left a trail of orchards in his wake on land he judged ripe for settlement. By the time settlers arrived, Chapman had trees ready for sale.

Chapman was an unlikely hero. Rough, barefoot, with no fixed address and often wearing little more than a sack and a pot on his head, Chapman emerged as a mythologized folk character suitable for children's tales in the late nineteenth century. The more peculiar aspects of his character, the stories concerning his arrangement with a frontier family to raise their ten-year-old daughter as his bride, or the ones about him pressing needles and hot coals into his feet, were glossed over. More than 300 books and plays on Chapman, by then more popularly known as Johnny Appleseed, were published between 1885 and 1950, as apples became the hyper-American fruit and Appleseed its hero.

Another well-known apple legend is no legend at all, since Isaac Newton told the story himself, although it may have been an exaggeration. One day in 1666, Newton observed an

Tradescant's Orchard, manuscript, 17th century.

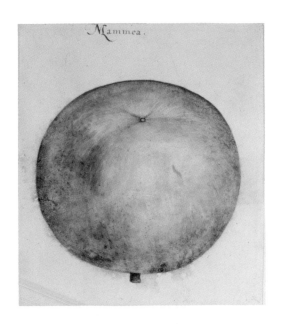

John White,
*Mammea Apple*,
*c.* 1580s.

apple fall from a tree in his orchard at Woolsthorpe, England. The apple's fall, he said, initiated the chain of thought that led him to the theory of gravity. Newton's admirers treated the event with such reverence that the story became the stuff of legend. Even the apple tree itself became legendary, coddled and protected until it finally fell, its remains carefully preserved. Seedling descendants of the famed tree have been planted at a few American universities including Tufts, the Massachusetts Institute of Technology and the University of Nebraska-Lincoln. Newton's story has even inspired a physics professor at Tufts to drop an apple on the heads of his graduating PhD students, hopefully inspiring new approaches to physics.

Apples are no stranger to popular culture today, either. Perhaps the most famous modern apple is 'The Big Apple', New York City. The catchphrase of John J. Fitz Gerald, track writer for the New York *Morning Telegraph* in the 1920s, it meant 'the big time', the place where big money could be won, in the racing parlance of the time. In a 1924 column, he wrote, 'The Big Apple. The dream of every lad that ever threw a leg over a thoroughbred and the goal of all horsemen. There's only one Big Apple. That's New York.' Fitz Gerald supposedly picked up the term from African-American stable hands at the racetrack in New Orleans. Charles Gillett, president of the New York Convention and Visitors Bureau, revived the phrase in the 1970s when seeking a new nickname for the city. The name stuck.

New York wasn't the only place that could have been called The Big Apple. Prior to the 1920s, several places in the United States and Canada were known as the 'Land of the Big (Red) Apple'. Oregon was one of the first to receive the nickname but at one time Missouri, Colorado, Washington and British Columbia also vied for the title.

Another famous modern apple belongs to a computer company. Steve Jobs came up with the name Apple for his company in 1976. At the time, he'd been spending a lot of time working and living on small farms, which is probably where he got the idea. Unable to come up with a better name, Jobs and his partners stuck with Apple. The company's first logo featured a picture of Isaac Newton sitting beneath his famous apple tree. Jobs thought the logo too detailed to be recognized on a computer, so he asked Rob Janoff to design a new logo in 1977. Janoff created the simple apple shape with the bite out of it still used today. The bite was said to have a double meaning: it symbolized the bite taken from the biblical fruit of knowledge as well as the unit of storage known as a byte in computer lingo.

The apple has managed to insinuate itself into every sort of human environment, from folklore and legends, to art,

Karl Anderson, *The Apple Gatherers*, 1912.

business and even common English idioms, such as 'upset the applecart' and 'the apple of one's eye'. Indicative of the fruit's tremendous range and adaptability, the apple has made itself at home in the soil and stories of cultures around the world, becoming the hero and message-bearer of its own remarkable story.

# 3
# Cider

Crush some apples, enough to release the juice, and an alchemical miracle takes place. The apple's clear, sugary juice quickly transforms into a cloudy brew that, left to its own devices, will fizz itself from sweet juice into a fermented brew.

In Europe and pre-Prohibition America, apples were more often drunk than eaten. Ralph Waldo Emerson went so far as to call apples the 'social fruit of New England' for its alcoholic virtues. The high esteem in which the apple was held in the seventeenth- and eighteenth-century American colonies and on the American frontier was due in large part to cider, one of the few safe beverages available to drink. Most households and taverns served cider rather than water, milk, wine, beer or most other hard liquors. Everyone from farmers to soldiers and political leaders drank cider. The habit had come to North America with the English, who had been drinking apples for centuries.

Cider was the alcoholic drink of choice in many of the northern regions of the world. Europe's three main cider-making areas – south-west England, north-west France and northern Spain – have cider traditions dating back to the Celts. The strongest drinks came from the sweetest fruits, and in the north, where grapes did not grow very well, that

John George Brown,
*Cider Mill*, 1880.

fruit was usually the apple. It also helped that cider was fairly easy to make. Anyone with a press and a barrel could make cider. Allowed to ferment for a few weeks, the pressed juice of apples produced an alcoholic beverage about half the strength of wine. For something stronger, the cider could be distilled into brandy or frozen into the intensely alcoholic drink known as applejack. The term 'hard cider', as alcoholic, fermented cider is often called in North America today, is a twentieth-century invention, as all cider was 'hard' until the advent of refrigeration made it possible to prevent sweet apple juice from fermenting.

No one really knows who first discovered cider, or even where in the world it was first made and consumed. This is due in part to the fact that apples are so widespread throughout the temperate areas of the globe. The first recorded reference to cider comes from the Romans. When Julius Cae invaded Britain in 55 BCE, he found Celts fermenting the juice of the island's native crab apples. The Celts weren't the only ones. The Romans reported that many of the European peoples they encountered produced several cider-like drinks, including some the Romans found superior to wines made from grapes. The Romans themselves had begun making perry, or pear cider, by the fourth century. Caesar's reputed fondness for cider might explain why the Romans worked so hard to improve their apple crops, eventually cultivating more than twenty varieties. Around the same time, St Jerome first used the word *sicera* to describe fermented apple juice, from which the word cider was derived. Sicera was related to the Greek word *sikera*, meaning simply 'intoxicating beverage', which was in turn taken from the Hebrew word *sekar* or *shekar*, which referred to any intoxicating beverage other than wine.

With the collapse of the Roman empire, the centre of horticultural arts shifted to Christian monastic orders and to the Islamic world. The Moors, who ruled Spain until the late fifteenth century, planted botanical gardens and used the gardening knowledge of the classical world to develop new techniques and apple varieties that would influence subsequent generations. They also created some of the classic bitter, high-tannin apples that still make some of the richest, most distinctive ciders today. Cider wasn't new to Spain, however, as people in northern Spain had made cider, or *sidra* as they called it, since before the birth of Christ on what may be the oldest apple-growing lands in Europe.

Cider-making developed gradually in north-western Europe. Charlemagne directed peasants to plant cider orchards and issued an edict encouraging cider-makers to develop their trade, yet cider-drinking took hold slowly. Even in Normandy, which would become one of the world's premier cider-making regions, cider was only widely consumed when beer was in short supply before the twelfth century. The Normans were sufficiently attracted to cider, though, to stir British interest after they conquered England in 1066.

Cider production spread from Normandy to other parts of France in the sixteenth and seventeenth centuries. French agricultural societies encouraged the production of cider, sponsoring cider-making competitions to entice more growers. Almost every farm producing cider also made cider brandy, a cider that's been distilled and then aged. The quality of the cider brandy produced in Calvados, a region in Normandy, became so legendary that the name 'Calvados' came to refer specifically to its cider brandy. It's been a subject of *appellation d'origine contrôlée* (AOC), the French system of specifying the geography and production methods of particular products to ensure quality, since 1942.

The outbreak of *phylloxera*, a tiny, aphid-like insect, which caused extensive damage to European grape stocks in the 1860s further stoked French enthusiasm for cider. Most of the great European winemakers had no choice but to replant their vineyards with insect-resistant American rootstocks. By the time the destruction to the grapes began to subside, an estimated four million apple trees were growing in France. Today, France is the biggest cider-maker in the world, with most production centred in Normandy and Brittany.

Cider and beer battled for dominance in English glasses throughout the Middle Ages. The Normans had introduced many new apple varieties to the island, including the pear-shaped Pearmain, the first named apple recorded in Britain, bolstering interest in cider-making. Cider lost some ground to beer in the fifteenth and sixteenth centuries, however, when hops came to England from Flanders. Hops improved the flavour of British ale as well as keeping it fresh for longer, making beer easier to store and easier to drink. Cider received another boost a century later, though, with the rise of Protestantism and the faith's high regard for the apple.

England's seventeenth-century farm economy fitted cider-making well. Apple trees were productive, low-maintenance and long-lived. Most cider apples didn't need to be harvested until October or later, when most other crops had been harvested and the farmer had time to press cider. Farm workers typically received a cider allowance as part of their wages, a practice that began in the thirteenth century and continued until 1878, when it was declared illegal.

Cider also made sense for England for two other reasons. First, England had a chronic shortage of burnable wood. Brewing beer required heat to malt the barley and boil the wort before fermentation; cider-making, on the other hand, required no heat and therefore no wood. Given the short supply of wood, planting fruit trees made good sense: young trees could provide apples for making cider while old trees could be burned for fuel. Second, Britain's shaky international relations with other European nations, particularly France and Germany, made cider-making a desirable way to lessen British dependence for its alcoholic beverages on potentially hostile countries. So for the English, cider made the most efficient use of resources as well as providing refreshment and a dash of patriotism.

Orchards and cider production had become firmly established in southern England by the eighteenth century, particularly in the counties of Gloucestershire, Somerset, Herefordshire, Worcestershire, Devonshire, Essex, Surrey, Sussex and Cornwall. The area's rich soils and mild, wet climate made it an ideal place to grow apples, a good thing since the English thirst for cider had grown prodigious by this time. Novelist Daniel Defoe reported that between 4.5 and 9 million litres (one and two million gallons) of cider

Lead-glazed earthenware jug, 1674. Large jugs to transport beer or cider were a constant need in rural communities.

were exported from the port of Exeter during the 1720s, while Londoners received bottles of cider from Hereford, in one of the country's most celebrated cider regions.

Wassailing the orchards, the practice of thanking the deity of the apple trees in order to ensure the next year's crop became an important practice in the English cider area. Held on the eve of Twelfth Night, 5 January, wassailing w regarded as essential to averting disaster in the orchard, though its origins are obscure and the tradition varies. In some places, a jug of cider or a piece of cider-soaked toast or cake was placed on the biggest apple tree to honour the gods. In others, the trees were sprinkled with cider. It was also important for a few small apples to be left on the tree for the pixies. A chant or song nearly always accompanied the offering, and the ceremony often concluded with the banging of kettles and pots, the firing of shots and the blowing of horns to either awake the tree gods or to scare away the evil spirits. Many orchards continue to wassail to this day.

Unfortunately, cider's popularity contributed to its decline in the mid-eighteenth century. Before then, cider-making had been a primarily rural activity, engaged in by farmers who made cider for home and local use, and by the wealthy who had the time and resources to invest in high-quality ciders. The Industrial Revolution changed everything: as more people moved from the farm to the city, the quality of cider dropped, although demand remained strong. Unscrupulous middlemen, eager to make a quick profit rather than a quality beverage, began selling adulterated or watered-down beverages that resembled cider in name only. Another drink, known as 'scrumpy', was made from just about anything that would ferment, including rotten fruit, vegetables and the juice of other fruits besides apples. Interestingly, the word scrumpy has become a positive descriptor, used today to distinguish ciders made in small batches using traditional methods (pure apple juice with nothing added and often cloudy in appearance) from mass-produced, industrial brands; in Britain, scrumpy is further delineated to refer to ciders from the West Country. Further damaging cider's reputation was the outbreak of Devonshire 'colic', a palsy-like illness caused by lead poisoning from the pipes of manufacturing

Dirk de Bray, 'A girl catched falling fruit in her apron as the boys climb the ladder', 1650–78, woodcut.

equipment. All of these degraded ciders made the new British ales like Guinness and Bass seem far more wholesome.

Industrialization changed English cider-making from small and local to large and commercial in the late nineteenth century. More than a dozen cider factories opened around Herefordshire between 1870 and 1900. One of these was H. P. Bulmer Ltd., founded in 1887 by Percy Bulmer, and today the largest cider-maker in the world, producing more than 60 per cent of the cider consumed in Britain.

As important as cider was in England, cider became even more integral to early American life. One in every ten farms in New England operated its own cider mill by the time of the American Revolution in the late eighteenth century. Even modest orchards could produce tremendous quantities of apples; cider-making allowed for the preservation of hundreds of bushels of apples in a small space. It quickly became America's national drink.

As in England, cider was seen as a healthy beverage to be served with every meal. It was also hygienic: even at low concentrations, alcohol kills most bacteria and viruses. Cider provided a trusted alternative to water at a time when most water was unpalatable or too polluted for everyone but the lucky few who lived near a natural, clear stream. Children drank cider cut with water while adults consumed mole-cider, a curious-sounding concoction of cider mixed with milk and a beaten egg, and cider soup, a concoction of cider thickened with flour and cream and sprinkled with croutons. President John Adams drank a tankard of cider every morning until he died, believing that it promoted good health. Cider was also used in the making of apple butter and applesauce, as well as for applejack and apple brandy. Cider vinegar proved essential to food preservation, used to pickle fruits and vegetables.

So plentiful was cider that barrels of it became its own barter currency, traded for everything from clothes to livestock to a child's schooling. An account book from New York in 1805 lists 'One half-barrel of cider for Mary's schooling'.

Although many areas of the United States produced cider, New Jersey became famed throughout the continent

Edward Calvert, *The Cyder Feast*, 1828, woodcut. Couples dance among the apple trees with a cider press in the background.

John Collier, 'A farmer sells apple cider and cherry cider in Massachusetts', 1941.

for both its ciders and its distilled apple brandies. The most celebrated came from Newark, where local apple varieties, including the Harrison, produced rich, sweet ciders that commanded high prices in New York. In 1810, Essex County, New Jersey, produced 198,000 barrels of cider and 1.2 million litres (307,310 gallons) of distilled cider spirits.

The great plantations of Virginia, including those of Presidents George Washington and Thomas Jefferson, were never without cider. Washington planted thousands of seedlings, experimented with grafting and became a major cider producer. Jefferson's epicurean proclivities kept him on a constant search for the best apples and the finest ciders. He planted two orchards at Monticello, one for fresh apples and one for cider apples. His favourite cider apple was said to be the Taliaferro (pronounced 'tolliver'), which yielded, he wrote, 'the finest cyder we have ever known, and more like wine than any liquor I have ever tasted which was not wine'.

As in England, the Industrial Revolution led to cidermaking's decline in America. The migration of workers from farms to cities and to the fertile lands of the West left many old orchards abandoned. Homemade cider didn't travel well, as it was unfiltered and unpasteurized. Moreover, a steady stream of new immigrants from Germany and northern Europe brought their beer-brewing culture with them to America, supplanting cider.

Most damaging to cider, however, was the rise of the Temperance movement in the nineteenth century. Cider, once considered wholesome and safe, became suspect and was placed alongside the 'demon rum' on the list of immoral intoxicants. Cider-makers themselves were partly to blame. For a long time, they had increased the alcohol content of

Cider press at Riley's farm in Oakglen, California.

cider (normally six per cent) with sweeteners to improve the keeping qualities of cider, especially cider intended for long-distance shipping. To give cider an extra boost, some cider makers added rum to the rough cider, producing cider that packed quite a punch. Applejack (made by freezing 'hard' cider outside in the winter) certainly didn't help bolster cider's cause, with its reputation for giving drinkers horrible hang-overs and a condition known as apple palsy. Finally, just as in England, dishonest manufacturers made inferior-quality ciders that sullied cider's good name.

Those sympathetic to the Temperance cause cut down their apple trees and swore off alcoholic beverages. By the time Prohibition became law in 1919, cider production in the United States had fallen to 50 million litres (13 million gallons), down from 210 million litres (55 million gallons) in 1899. Prohibition also changed the language. The word cider came to mean unfermented sweet apple juice in America, produced from surplus apples, rather than the beverage that had sustained and nourished the country's founding genera-tions of settlers.

Once Prohibition ended, cider, unlike beer, never came back. Where apple trees could take ten years to produce fruit, barley and hops could be grown and harvested quickly to meet surging demand. To make cider, orchardists had to care-fully graft apple trees or spend years tending a new orchard from seed to have the raw material necessary for cider. Beer was also big business. Beer-makers had lobbied hard for the repeal of Prohibition to save their industry. Cider-makers, on the other hand, traditionally produced cider in small batches and worked independently, so they didn't have the same business incentive and industrial heft that drove brewers.

In recent years, though, cider has begun to experience a re-naissance of sorts as demand for cider is growing in America,

Scheffer & Beck, Kickok's patent cider mill, 1850.

in Europe and around the world. Small orchardists and cider-makers are once again experimenting with different varieties of apples to find the best ones for making cider. Good cider, like wine, is a balance of acid, tannin and other flavours that result from fermentation.

While cider can technically be produced from any apple available, the best ciders come from blends of mellow, acidic and bitter apples. Nearly any apple, from puckeringly tart crabs to sugary sweet apples, will add something to a cider blend; good cider is rarely made from just one variety.

Apples can be divided into three broad categories that roughly correspond to taste and use: dessert, cooking and cider apples. Dessert apples are usually eaten fresh out of hand and are sweet in flavour but balanced with acidity. Cooking apples often taste more tart because they have more malic acid (the active ingredient in most sour or tart foods) or because they have less sugar. They also tend to cook down into a softy, pulpy mass rather than retaining their shape like dessert apples.

Cider apples are the most arbitrary category of fruit, since both dessert and cooking apples are used to make cider. True cider apples are bitter and astringent from the tannins found in the skin and flesh of the fruit. Tannin, also found in the skin of wine grapes, stabilizes and clarifies the cider. It contributes a spicy aroma and gives body and a dry finish to both cider and wine. Tannins also increase the keeping qualities of finished cider. Cider apples can be further divided into four types: bittersweet (high tannin, low acid), sweet (low tannin, low acid), bittersharp (high tannin, high acid) and sharp (low tannin, high acid). The blending of these apples can take place when the apples are grinded before pressing, after pressing or after fermentation. Each blending method produces its own distinct qualities.

The basic method of turning apples into cider has changed little over the past centuries. Fruits are harvested and then 'sweated' in storage to release excess water and ethylene gas, and to allow the starches in the flesh to turn to sugar. The fruit is then ground, pressed and fermented. Unlike wine, most ciders don't need long-term ageing before they are ready to drink. Most should be ready within six months.

Different apple-growing regions of the world produce distinctive styles of cider. Regional variations depend on available apples, local methods and local tastes. The Pays d'Auge

# TREE OF INTEMPERANCE
### BY A. D. FILLMORE

A. D. Fillmore, 'Tree of Intemperance', 1855. This print expounds on the benefits of temperance and the evils of drink. A serpent with an apple in its mouth and a mug of beer on its head is wrapped around a gnarled tree with roots of schnapps, whiskey, wine, beer and other spirits.

area of Normandy has produced sparkling cider since the thirteenth century. The bubbles come from sugar added to the cider before it is poured into thick bottles, capped and stored upright like champagne. Ciders in Switzerland and

Germany are usually made from surplus dessert apples. Known as *Apfelwein*, these ciders resemble white wine more than the rich, full-bodied ciders of Britain. In northern Spain, where cider has been made for thousands of years, small, regional cider-makers buy apples from local farmers and sell their cider to local cider bars. Usually unlabelled, the only way to identify the cider-maker is to look for the stamp on the cork. The country's largest cider-maker, El Gaitero, makes a sweet sparkling cider, although the traditional Spanish cider is dry, tart and effervescent. English cider-makers vary in size from the small cider mills to the large Bulmer's, and make ciders that are sweeter and higher in alcohol than French cider.

Even with all of the variety, ciders do fall into some broad categories. Draught cider, the most common of commercial ciders, is made from the juice of surplus dessert apples fermented to dryness. This produces cider with a much higher alcohol level than natural, unsweetened cider. These fermentations are then filtered and blended with water and/or apple juice to lower the alcohol content to around six per cent. Draught ciders are usually sweet and best drunk cold. Sparkling cider is cider that has been carbonated in some way, sometimes naturally through bottled fermentation or alternatively by means of carbon-dioxide injection.

Farmhouse cider, also known as traditional cider, is usually still, dry and fully fermented to 5 per cent alcohol. French cider is a light, lower-alcohol cider that can be either effervescent or still. This cider has had its fermentation arrested by a process known as defecation in which the pectins, tannins, yeasts and nutrients are precipitated out of the fresh cider before it begins a long, slow fermentation. Another variety, known as cyser, has honey added as a sweetening agent. The last category, speciality ciders, covers a wide range of beverages, including those that contain the juice from other fruits and those flavoured with almost anything a cider-maker can imagine.

Cider's resurgence in popularity has brought forth a new-found appreciation of the apple, not unlike that of micro-brewers for forgotten beer styles. In America, 'hard' cider consumption increased twenty-fold between 1987 and 1997. Many new cideries have opened on the east and west coasts and in the Upper Midwest. The British consume more than 460 million litres (100 million gallons) of cider annually, four times the amount of cider consumed in the 1960s. The vast majority of that cider comes from large industrial cidermakers like Bulmers, which is based in Hereford. Herefordshire is also home to the Cider Museum, which covers every aspect of British cider-making, as well as the Cider Route, a path that takes visitors to cider-makers throughout the county that collectively produce more than half of Britain's cider. While cider may likely never again reach the pride of place it once held in rural England and colonial America, it's comforting to know that something as ancient as cidermaking remains alive and well.

# 4
# Wholesome Apple

An apple a day didn't always keep the doctor away. In fact, for many centuries in Europe, eating a fresh apple was almost a sure reason to call for the doctor. Apples in medieval Europe were banned for children and wet nurses. They were also among the chief suspects in any case of upset stomach, flux (dysentery) or flu. Apples didn't become symbols of health and wholesomeness until the late nineteenth century, when apple growers launched a public relations campaign to encourage the consumption of the fresh fruit over alcoholic cider.

Apples played a major medicinal role in the classical world. They were ascribed different healing powers depending on the type of apple. Some apples could be both astringents and diuretics. Apples could cure any sort of bellyache, and the smell of apples could supposedly prevent vomiting. Poultices for cardiac diseases and fevers nearly always contained apples. Other apples were thought to relieve arthritis and sciatica; to provide an antidote to poison; and to relieve birthing pain.

The digestive qualities associated with apples were one reason that apples commonly appeared at the end of Roman meals. The second-century Greek physician Galen as well as his medical and philosophical predecessors such as Hippocrates believed that the human body was composed of four elements or humours: blood, phlegm, and black and yellow bile. These elements were hot, cold, dry and moist respectively, and were associated with different human temperaments and disorders. Foods also fell into this classification system, giving physicians a system for determining when and how various foods should be eaten in order to maintain or correct the balance of the humours. Apples fell into the cool and moist category, a counterbalance to the heat of main meal foods like red meat.

These wholesome qualities only extended to cultivated apples, however. Sour crab apples were seen as unhealthy, although they did have some specific medicinal applications, including the treatment of fainting and constipation.

Ancient beliefs about apples had a profound influence on how apples were viewed for centuries. The teachings of the twelfth-century medical school in Salerno, Italy, considered the cradle of Western medical education, promulgated the therapeutic applications of apples for disturbances of the bowels, lungs and nervous systems. They published many of their dietary and pharmaceutical rules and advice in poem form in a book called *Regimen Sanitatis* or *Prescription for Health*, which was the most popular health and cure book in the Middle Ages. The Salerno school's teachings initiated a tradition of apple cures that continued into the nineteenth century.

Seventeenth-century home cures also commonly included apples. This reliance on apples for healing didn't mean that the fresh fruit was safe to eat for enjoyment, though; rather, fresh apples had specific medicinal purposes. Doctors and healers prescribed a cup of cider for depression, although it may have been the alcohol that provided the real cheering. The Elizabethan herbalist John Gerard recommended a poultice of apples for swelling and wrote that 'the pulp of roasted apples mixed to a froth in water and drunk by the quart, has benefited those with gonorrhoea'. Victorian farm workers soaked rags in cider vinegar to relieve their aches and pains, and chapped skin received a thick coating of lard and chopped apples.

The classical distrust of sour apples continued into the Middle Ages, extending even, in some cases, to the more edible specimens. Since eating sour fruit and overindulging in the sweet variety could both cause gastric distress, some caution was warranted. As late as 1541, English author and administrator Sir Thomas Elyot warned that 'All fruits are generally noyful to man, and do engender ill humour, and be oft times the cause of putrefied fevers.' The decline of Roman orchards after the fall of their empire left bitter fruit that fed the notion that apples were poisonous. Even though people continued to eat fruit, suspicions about its wholesomeness were not unfounded. Fruits sold in village and city marketplaces were often unripe, overripe or contaminated by the insects and rodents that swarmed around open cesspools.

Unease with the apple may also have had something to do with its identification as the cause of Eve's downfall. Artistic depictions of the event often showed Adam and Eve beneath an unmistakable apple tree, certainly enough to give would-be consumers pause.

Cooking apples seemed to calm some uneasiness, however. A fourteenth-century Italian medical treatise mentions that heat and spice offset the apple's cold, negative properties. It also points out that apples taste better cooked, especially when sprinkled with sugar and served with candied anise. Roasted apples or pears eased digestion at the end of English meals in the fourteenth century.

For certain ailments, raw apples were acceptable. During Lent, ten raw apples a day kept English monks regular. An apple eaten raw at the beginning of a meal would open the stomach and stimulate the heart, though they were still considered quite harmful to nerves, so the consumer had to decide whether an open stomach was worth the risk.

Another advantage of apples recognized in the Middle Ages was that an apple eaten after a meal could clean teeth. While not a substitute for a toothbrush, apples are still considered a good teeth-cleansing food today.

Even if raw apples were not necessarily safe to ingest in the Middle Ages, apples played a prominent role in the medieval pharmacy. Apple pulp provided the vehicle for many medicines applied externally, as well as for some beauty products. The origin of the word pomade, the waxy substance used to style hair, also traces its origins to apple pulp.

During the age of European exploration in the fifteenth, sixteenth and seventeenth centuries, apples helped to ameliorate the disastrous effects of scurvy on ship voyages. Captain

Medicinal vase, c. 1515, tin-glazed earthenware. Storage jar for various medicinal herbs, roots, syrups, pills, ointments and sweetmeats common during the Middle Ages.

James Cook carried Hunt Hall apples for his men and is reported never to have lost a man from scurvy. British whaling ships in the ninteenth century, whose crews could be away for long periods of time, stocked the ship with apples and barrels of cider. Every ship company embarking on long voyages soon learned of the apple's anti-scorbutic qualities, and the apple, along with lemons and limes, became one of the few fruits to travel the high seas.

Suspicion of eating raw fruit didn't begin to lift in England until the sixteenth century, in part, due to the spread of sugar. Sugar had been known to the Mediterranean world since at least 325 BCE, when Alexander the Great's admiral Nearchos reported seeing sugar in India. But for centuries, sugar was used as a medicine rather than a sweetener. The Romans mixed sugar with spices and used it as a warming medicine good for treating the bowels, kidneys, stomach and bladder. The Persians and then the Arabs pioneered the growing and refining of sugar on a large scale, using sugar in cooking as well as medicine.

The combination of fruit and sugar in medicine was logical. Sugar was not only a warming spice that could counteract the believed cold properties of fruit, but was also a less variable substance than the more common European sweetener, honey. Sugar could also make a sterile syrup that could prevent spoilage and whose strength could be controlled. Sugar could preserve fruit in jams, jellies or crystallized form as well.

These preserved fruits were first used to deliver the therapeutic properties of fruit rather than to make sweets, however. The first recipes for fruit pastes, sweets, jams and syrups are found in Arab pharmacopoeias, rather than cookbooks. As sugar became cheaper and more widely available, a final, lavish dessert-course of fruit emerged in Europe, further shifting attitudes about eating fresh fruit towards the positive.

National Apple Week Association float in front of the Pan American Union, Washington, DC, 1926. Note the promotion of the apple as healthy in the banner. National Apple Week began in 1904 to increase consumer awareness and interest in apples.

More people were eating raw fruit without becoming unwell, which helped shift medical and popular opinion on apples. The steady increase in the number of good eating varieties also helped apples' standing as a safe and delicious raw fruit.

Even so, apples were still more often drunk than eaten, especially in rural England and colonial America. At a time when water quality was poor and milk unpasteurized, cider was an inexpensive, safe drink that nearly anyone could – and did – make. Cider was safe even for children, who were given watered-down cider as a nutritious, wholesome beverage.

That view of cider's healthful benefits changed radically in the nineteenth century with the American Temperance movement, however. As America moved away from agriculture and toward urbanization, many people became alarmed by the changes they saw around them: extreme poverty, disease and crime, among others. Temperance supporters came to believe that the cause of most social problems could be found in alcohol. Some farmers cut down their apple trees, while others simply stopped producing alcoholic beverages altogether in favour of sweet apple juice. Temperance created a market for this non-alcoholic juice, further encouraged by

Apples were recommended to children as part of a healthy school lunch.

followers such as the Reverend Sylvester Graham, Presbyterian preacher, Temperance lecturer and self-styled diet guru. Graham claimed that 'fruits, vegetables and nuts make for temperance', that food was more healthful the less it was cooked and asked rhetorically, 'what luxuries can compare with the luscious peach, or the juicy apple?' As Americans began to see diet as not only the key to physical health but moral heath, the foundations of a modern health food movement were established.

To save apples from the hatchets of the Temperance advocates, the apple industry launched a public relations campaign to reposition the fruit as healthful rather than harmful. At the 1904 World's Fair in St Louis, J. T. Stinson, a Missouri fruit specialist, coined the famous adage 'an apple a day keeps the doctor away', an association that apples have benefited from ever since.

Today, when apples are universally thought of as healthy, it can be hard to believe that apples once aroused suspicion. Apples contain fibre, vitamins and flavonoids that play an important role in preventing many types of disease and in promoting good digestion. That apples are available nearly year-round also makes them an easy, healthy choice.

# 5
# Global Apple

Apples are one of the most widely grown and eaten fruit in the world. In North America alone, some 14,000 apple varieties have been named and nurtured over the last four centuries, and thousands more are known worldwide. But despite the apple's astounding diversity of flavours, colours, shapes and uses worldwide, the vast majority of apple varieties are never seen for sale, even at small orchards. Conservative estimates suggest that fewer than one in ten of the apple varieties grown in the past remain commercially available. What happened to all the apples?

The answer lies in the apple's transition from a local speciality to a global commodity. The modern apple industry has grown so large that only twenty or so apples have gained a place at the global table – and nearly all of them are varieties first developed in North America. This transition began in the nineteenth century as industrialization, new technology and advances in transportation began to radically change the organization of food production and distribution for people all over the world. In an era often defined by rushes and entrepreneurial energy, especially in Europe and North America, even apples could be a source of riches.

Arthur Rothstein, 'Workers at apple packinghouse in Camden County, New Jersey', 1938.

Sea transport made it possible for the United States, Canada, Australia, New Zealand and eventually South Africa to send barrel after barrel of fresh apples abroad in the nineteenth century. Whereas before apples for export had traditionally been dried or made into cider, improved ships plus new, hardier apple varieties led to a huge increase in the transport of fresh fruit. Competition between these apple-growing regions encouraged growers to focus on a handful of good commercial varieties, usually one or two types per grower, that could be produced in large quantities and could survive overseas travel intact.

Apple-breeding flourished in the late eighteenth and early nineteenth centuries as growers rushed to find the perfect apple for an expanding global marketplace. Innovative farmers and growers began to correspond and share plants, even before the growth of global trade. London publisher Samuel

Hartlib, for example, networked with many agricultural inventors, including German physician Johann Brun, who helped to introduce several new apple types to England in the seventeeth century. Sharing findings and seedlings helped northern growers in particular, many of who were eager to find apples that could grow well in extreme climates. The biggest breakthroughs in apple-breeding, however, happened once the apple took root in North America.

American growers in the nineteenth century exhibited a single-minded dedication to the pursuit of commercial varieties. Johnny Appleseed and his wild seedlings may have had their place in home orchards for cider and as feed for hogs, but serious growers knew it was no way to stake a fortune. With nearly unlimited space, Americans began developing orchards filled with grafted trees carefully chosen by enterprising nurserymen. From these orchards came unique American apples like Baldwin, Green Newton, Jonathan, Hawley, Spitzenburg, Winesap and York Imperial, many of which became extremely popular to grow and eat in Europe.

American growers also benefited from the continent's geographic advantages. New York, with its deep harbour and

*An* apple orchard in the winter.

position on the Hudson River, became a major exporting centre, shipping apples grown in nearby states as well as encouraging the planting of orchards along the Hudson River itself. Americans were exporting apples to the West Indies by 1741. Less than twenty years later, in 1758, the first transatlantic shipment of American apples occurred when Benjamin Franklin received a supply of Newtown Pippins while serving as the Pennsylvania agent to the British government. Franklin promptly shared the fruit with a friend, initiating a brisk apple trade between London and the Philadelphia supplier.

Apple breeding and production increased steadily across North America throughout the second half of the nineteenth century. Plant breeders, especially in the American Midwest, looked to Russia for apple varieties that might grow well in a cold climate, especially after famed American newspaper editor Horace Greeley told an 1860 audience, 'Never move to Minnesota . . . You can't grow apples there!' Fortunately for Minnesota and the rest of the American Midwest, breeder Peter Gideon's discovery of the hardy 'Wealthy' apple in the late 1860s, a variety with Russian parentage, encouraged the breeding of more cold-tolerant apples in the United States. Soon, the University of Minnesota received about 150 Russian apple varieties for testing and grafting, and apple trees spread across the Midwest and all the way to the Pacific coast.

In Canada, Charles Arnold of Paris, Ontario, became the first to crossbreed apples. He exhibited eighteen varieties at the 1873 meeting of the American Pomological Society. One became the fairly well-known Ontario apple. Arnold's work encouraged other Canadian apple growers, and soon apples were among the nation's most valuable agricultural industries, grown primarily in British Columbia and Ontario.

Russia, too, developed a thriving fruit-breeding programme in the late nineteenth and early twentieth centuries.

Despite having no formal scientific training or ties to an academic or research institution, Ivan Vladimirovich Michurin (1855–1935) became one of the country's leading breeders, seeking to find fruit that would thrive in a harsh climate. Michurin had his own unique breeding technique, believing he could acclimatize seedlings in order to transmit their cold-hardiness to any new plants from their seeds. Using this method, Michurin created several apple hybrids as well as crosses between apples and pears and between apples and hawthorns. By 1919, Michurin had bred 153 new fruit varieties, including 45 kinds of apples. He also created five kinds of cold-tolerant kiwi, which were introduced to the United States and are now among the most widely grown type in the world. Michurin's work led to the creation of 14 research institutes across Russia in different growing zones, as well as more than 100 smaller centres in northern areas that aim at the development of hardy fruit types.

As the agricultural market grew larger and more global, the small market gardeners with their diverse orchards could not compete. Many local, favourite apples simply ceased to be grown because their irregular crops, tendency to bruising or disease or other shortcomings failed to meet the stringent requirements of the new global marketplace.

Commercial apples now had to be pretty and crisp, even after weeks or months spent in transit and in storage. Growers competed fiercely to produce the most attractive rather than the most delicious fruit as taste took a back seat to the needs of export shipping. The changes in the apple market were noticeable even in the nineteenth century. American writer Henry David Thoreau commented: 'Apples for grafting appear to have been selected commonly, not so much for their spirited flavor, as for their mildness, their size, and bearing qualities – not so much for their beauty, as for their fairness and soundness.' The market's devotion to crispness and beauty as essential marks of a good modern apple removed any idea of seasonality from an apple's taste and texture: a hard measure for many delicious but temperamental older, regional apple varieties to meet.

The race to breed the best apple was (and continues to be) as brisk as the race for any other technological marvel. Some 8,000 apples have been specially bred in research centres and national orchards worldwide. In the United States, the establishment of the American Pomological Society in 1852 spurred apple research and the expansion of orchard lands by providing a clearing-house for information on apple-growing. The British founded their own Pomological Society in 1854 to compete with the Americans. Many of the important apple rootstocks used to develop new varieties came from the East Malling Research Station in Kent, England, in the early 1900s. Researchers there collected and characterized rootstocks developed by farmers over many centuries in Europe,

Newly harvested apples ready for shipping.

providing a strong foundation for carrying forth desired traits into future apple types. East Malling has also developed many unique apple types, including Greensleeves, Meridian and Fiesta. Cornell University's Experimental Research Station in Ithaca, New York, runs one of the largest apple-breeding programmes in the world. More than 60 apple varieties, including such common apples as the Empire, Cortland and Jonagold, have been created there since its founding in the 1890s. Since the 1930s, the University of Minnesota has introduced a steady stream of hardy apples that can withstand cold winters and hot, dry summers including the Fireside, Regent, State Fair, Honeygold, Zester and the increasingly popular Honeycrisp. Japan's Amori Apple Experiment Station started breeding apples in 1929 and has produced eight patented types, including Mutsu (known as Crispin in the UK).

Apple varieties developed in North America were planted in orchards around the world and now account for more than 80 per cent of the world's apple market. American apples helped kickstart the apple industry in South America, South Africa and Asia.

Apples have a long history in Asia, though until the late nineteenth century most of the commonly found apples were small and sharply flavoured, and were used for preserves rather than eaten fresh. The first recorded reference to apples in Korea, for example, dates from AD 1103, but only royalty and the upper classes could afford to eat them until 1906, when the Korean government started investing in sweet apple cultivation. The introduction of large, sweet Western apples by missionaries in the late nineteenth and early twentieth centuries caused apple production to soar in Asia and allowed more people to enjoy the fruit in new ways. Apples are now a major industry in Turkey, India and Iran, but most are consumed locally.

The Japanese apple industry developed after the importation of 75 American apple cultivars in 1871. Crosses of these American apples resulted in several new Japanese apple types, including the Fuji apple, a cross between a Red Delicious and a Ralls Jennet, introduced in 1962. Apple-breeding became very popular in Japan in the twentieth century and the Fuji apple an essential parent for many other new apple types. Japan did not open its market to apple imports until 1971.

The Chinese government initiated China's apple boom in the 1980s as the country started opening its agriculture to the world market and investing in improved productivity and quality. Although the Chinese have known how to graft for thousands of years, the large sweet apples that became so beloved in the West took much longer to become common in China. It's difficult to know when sweet apples first appeared in China because references to apples in historic texts could

Ji-Ho Oh, *Apple Orchard*, 1937.

refer to the country's indigenous bitter, small-fruited species. In the 1970s, common Chinese apples were relatively small and tasteless, unfit for sale on the world market. But Chinese apples improved significantly when the government began importing Red and Yellow Delicious seedlings from the US and enhanced the quality of local varieties like the Guoguan and Jinguan. China now produces more than 1.5 billion US bushels of apples a year, about half the world's supply and nearly seven times the amount grown in America. Many of those apples end up as juice concentrate.

In South America, Chile has become one of the largest fruit producers in the world, accounting for nearly half of the fruit grown in the southern hemisphere and one-third of that hemisphere's apple production. Spanish and Portuguese explorers and missionaries brought apples to South America in the seventeenth and eighteenth centuries. The apple flourished in its new home, quickly escaping from cultivation in Jesuit orchards and establishing itself throughout the valleys of Argentina and Chile. Basilio Villarino, captain of the Spanish Royal Navy, described land covered in apple trees and bartering with Indians for apples weighing more than 450 g (1 lb) during his 1782–3 expedition up the Rio Negro in Patagonia. Argentina, Chile and Brazil began exporting apples in large quantities in the 1980s, most of which went to the US and Europe. The opposition in seasons between the northern and southern hemispheres that brings South American apples to market during the winter months in the north has contributed to the tremendous growth in southern hemisphere apple production. Chile mostly grows red apples for export, including the Gala, Fuji and Braeburn varieties.

In the USA, the state of Washington has been the largest producer since the 1920s. Every year, Washington exports

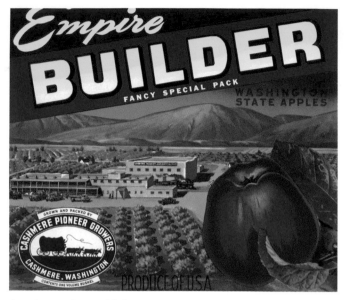

American apple crate labels, 1910–20s.

around 30 per cent of their apples to more than 60 countries around the world. The apple has become so iconic to the state that the football game between the University of Washington and Washington State is played for the Apple Cup, and the state is sometimes referred to as the 'apple state'. New York, Michigan, Pennsylvania and California are other top apple-producing states.

Worldwide production of apples now runs into the many millions of tons. Unsurprisingly, the world's largest apple producers are also the world's largest consumers of apples. Americans eat an average of 7.7 kg (17 lb) of apples per person a year, and the fruit is second only to bananas in popularity. Italy, France, Poland and Germany lead apple-production in Europe. Europeans eat an average of 18.1 kg (40 lb) of apples per person a year, and more in apple-producing

# America's Delight

### NORTHWEST
## APPLES

GROWN & PACKED FOR
**NORTH PACIFIC
SALES CO.**
SEATTLE
U.S.A.

# Lake WENATCHEE
BRAND

## APPLES

PACKED & SHIPPED BY
CASCOA GROWERS
CASHMERE, WASH.

regions where apples are integral to local food traditions. The Chinese consume upwards of 13.6 kg (30 lb) per person.

In the twentieth century breeders began patenting their apples; Cortland, Jonagold, Gala, Fuji and Honeycrisp all have patents. When a tree is patented, nurseries selling that variety charge a royalty on each tree sold to repay the breeders for development costs. In the USA, patent law does not require the holder to sell the apples to the public, while in New Zealand patent-holders must sell to the public after three years, though there is no penalty for ignoring the obligation. Agricultural patents last only seventeen years, at which point the cultivars are free for anyone to grow. Because it takes up to ten years to bring new trees into production, patent-holders have only a short window in which to prosper. Trademarks, on the other hand, can be renewed indefinitely. New Zealand, where the Braeburn apple was developed in the 1940s, became the first nation to trademark the names of its apples. This means that while anyone can grow a Braeburn cultivar, they can't call it by that name without paying a fee.

Some of the apples most commonly known and eaten today are the Red Delicious, Golden Delicious, Granny Smith, McIntosh, Rome Beauty, Fuji, Jonathan, York, Gala, Idared and Cortland apples. Of these, the Fuji and Gala, as well as a few other rising apple stars such as Jonagold, Elstar and Empire, are the offspring of the major international varieties developed in the nineteenth century. Conventional apple-breeding has long concentrated on a very small number of cultivars to develop new apple varieties. The Pink Lady apple, for example, is a cross of the Golden Delicious and the Lady Williams. The Jonagold is a cross of the Jonathan and Golden Delicious, and the Gala is a cross of Kidd's Orange Red and the Golden Delicious.

The most widely eaten apple variety in the world is the Golden Delicious, accounting for more than 65 per cent of

Golden Delicious is the most widely eaten apple in the world.

the world market. An estimated 60 per cent of commercial apples grown in France are Golden Delicious. Discovered as a seedling on Anderson Mullins's farm in West Virginia around 1890, Mullins watched the tree until 1914 when he sent some fruit, which he named Mullins Yellow Seedling, to Stark Brothers Nursery in Missouri. Paul Stark, sufficiently impressed with the fruit, came to inspect the tree, which he bought and renamed the Golden Delicious. Golden Delicious was extensively planted around the US by the 1920s, and became the archetype of the modern commercial apple. It's easy to grow, regularly shaped and a heavy producer, all factors that made it ideally suited for supermarkets that demand a uniform, consistent product.

Red Delicious has been the favourite in the us but its popularity is declining.

Another Delicious, the Red Delicious, is the most popular apple in America, constituting nearly a quarter of the entire apple crop in the United States, though its popularity is on the decline. Its characteristic profile, long with five prominent bumps at the base, has been immortalized as the logo of Washington-grown apples since the 1960s. Its characteristic bland, cottony flavour has also been embedded into public perceptions of the apple, leading to its decline in recent years.

It wasn't always this way. The original Red Delicious, found growing on Jesse Hiatt's farm near Peru, Iowa, had a

sweet flavour and perfumed aroma. It wasn't the deep, uniformly red colour we know today, but rather was streaked
with shades of red and yellow. Hiatt, already the developer of
the Hiatt Sweet and Hiatt Black apples, tried to kill the tree
several times, but each year the root sent up new shoots. He
finally decided to let it grow, and when it bore its first fruit
in 1872 he fell in love with it and named it the 'Hawkeye'.
Twenty-two years later, Clarence M. Stark of the Stark Brothers Nursery, the same nursery that commercialized Golden
Delicious, chose Hiatt's apple as the best in the nation from
entries submitted in a contest to find an apple to replace the
popular Ben Davis. Stark bought the rights to propagate the
Hawkeye, renamed it Delicious, and spent nearly one million
dollars promoting it to growers. When Stark's successors
found and named the Golden Delicious in 1914, the Delicious
became Red Delicious. By the Second World War the Red
Delicious had become America's favourite apple, bred now
for its iconic appearance and durability rather than its flavour.
The Red Delicious has been extensively used in breeding programmes, serving as the parent of such popular apples as the
Fuji, Empire and Cameo.

The world's most common green apple, the Granny Smith,
originated in what is now the Sydney suburb of Eastwood,
Australia. Mrs Maria Ann Smith, a real granny, discovered the
seedling growing by a creek on her farm in 1868 where she
had once discarded some French crab apples. Smith died
before the apple that eventually bore her name achieved commercial success, but local orchardists continued to cultivate
the fruit. Exhibited at an 1891 agricultural show in Australia,
the apple took first prize, and four years later was named a
suitable variety for export by the Australian government. The
Granny Smith apple is today extensively grown in the southern hemisphere. It's particularly popular for export due to its

waxy skin and robust, crisp flavour. While she may not have lived to see her apple achieve worldwide fame, Mrs Smith herself was not forgotten. A site near her home was named Granny Smith Memorial Park in 1950, and in 1985 the first annual Granny Smith Festival was held.

The bestselling apple in Canada is, unsurprisingly, a variety discovered in Canada: the McIntosh apple. John McIntosh discovered a group of apple trees growing on his property in Dundela, Ontario, in 1811. He transplanted the trees to a location closer to his home, and one produced what became the McIntosh apple. McIntosh's son Allan established a nursery and extensively promoted the species.

The development of these iconic commercial apples changed the apple industry as well as the way apples are grown. Today, apple-growing is a highly specialized enterprise, intensively managed and scientifically studied. Government-funded training and research centres devoted to fruit were established

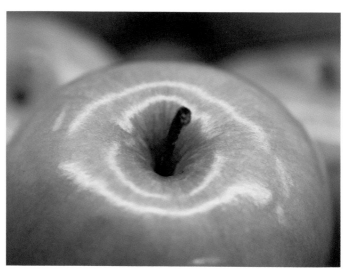

Granny Smith is a native of Australia.

Paul Cézanne, *Green Apples*, c. 1873.

in the mid- to late nineteenth century in North America, New Zealand, Australia and Europe. Asian counties soon followed suit. These research institutes tackled everything from rootstocks and pest control to storage and the chemistry of ripening. Growers, too, aligned themselves with the latest research in biological sciences, passing the work of the breeding and evaluation of apples from amateur breeders and backyard orchardists into the hands of professionals.

Since the 1970s, most apple-growers have switched to dwarf trees that bear fruit within five years as compared to eight to ten years or more for the standard tree. These dwarf trees give an early return on investment, are more easily managed and make the most efficient use of space, important qualities for the global marketplace. The most intensive modern orchards packed with dwarf trees grow 1,300 trees per acre rather than the standard 48 for regular trees. Orchards

Spring apple blossoms.

are not so old as they once were, either. Where once orchards used to produce fruit for 50 years or more, whole orchards are now replaced every ten to fifteen years so growers get the benefit of young, healthy trees. Apple trees are also shaped and trained by orchardists to maximize the amount of light the tree receives in order to increase production.

Pesticides and insecticides have also changed the apple industry. Chemicals were not widely used in apple-growing in North America until the late nineteenth century because many of the pests that would eventually become troublesome had not yet made the trip to the New World. Public perceptions of how fruit should look also discouraged pesticide use: some pest damage was accepted as natural and unavoidable. Most people saw no problem with bumpy, discoloured and pock-marked apples. Still-life paintings of fruit from before the nineteenth century clearly show insect damage and disease. Pesticides were introduced to the orchard once growers began producing more fruit for market and fresh eating rather than for cider and home consumption. The first arsenical insectide, Paris green, was developed in the 1870s to control the codling moth, a pest accidentally brought by settlers from Europe. By 1945, orchardists used up to seven applications of lead arsenate each season. Following the Second World War, DDT was used with increasing frequency.

Public concern over pesticides led to the introduction of integrated pest management in the 1970s, a system that places a greater emphasis on understanding the life cycle of pests and other diseases. In this system, crops are sprayed in accordance with these cycles rather than as matter of course as in the past, reducing pesticide use and frequency of application. Pesticide use on apples remains higher than on most other

Pest damage such as this was common and acceptable for apples in the past.

crops as fruit growers strive to meet marketplace demands for inexpensive, blemish-free fruit.

Improvements in storage methods also proved pivotal to the growth of the apple industry. Huge profits could be made by storing and transporting perishable goods, so many countries invested major research initiatives into studying how best to store and handle fruit in the nineteenth century. The first step was to understand how it ripened.

As living, breathing organisms, apples begin to deteriorate as soon as they are picked. An apple eaten today won't taste or smell quite the same as it would have done the day before, a liability for growers. Fully grown apples release a chemical called ethylene that stimulates the ripening process and eventually leads to its decay. Cold storage keeps apples fresh by slowing down the production of ethylene, something apple growers had known even if they didn't understand the process for centuries. Prior to refrigeration, apples were commonly packed in barrels and buried underground to keep them cool, or stored in root cellars. By controlling the storage atmosphere, scientists found that newly harvested apples could be maintained close to the condition at which they were picked, a major advancement for the industry. The development of the refrigerated railroad car in the late nineteenth century and of cold storage in the early twentieth allowed apples to be kept fresher for longer and longer periods over greater distances. Today, the science of storage has grown so sophisticated that researchers can now chemically analyse apples to determine how long they can be stored at near harvest quality.

Many people argue that this control of ripening has resulted in apples that are simultaneously unripe and past their prime. An apple picked before it is ready can often be mealy, its bright skin promising something its flesh can't deliver. But it is this process that enables supermarket chains to demand

Tree markers distinguish the hundreds of varieties grown in this orchard in Iowa, 2009.

– and receive – the same narrow range of apple varieties all year long. Controlled ripening has also changed perceptions of the fruit, which used to be thought of according to its seasonal qualities, from the refreshing, light and crisp summer apples to the richer, spicier autumn and winter apples. Today's apples must be crisp and sweet year-round to find a place in the global supermarket.

Consumer rebellion against intensively produced food products in recent years has led to efforts to try and regain the world's apple heritage. Many older varieties are being rediscovered and planted in gardens and parks, and on the grounds of historic sites. Around 34 per cent of National Parks in the United States have historic orchards in them. Apples themselves remain a determined and subversive force. In the orchards of abandoned homesteads in New England,

Seed Savers Historic Orchard, 2009. Antique apple trees filled with autumn fruit.

along ancient pathways of England, and in the fields and other marginal lands of the temperate world, seedling apples of unknown parentage continue to grow. As in the past, many of these apples are of little edible value (though great for pigs), but every so often, a rare, delicious individual apple emerges. The list of apples available from nurseries continues to grow and groups have formed around the world to study and increase public awareness of heritage apples. Local markets and regional agriculture have also helped raise awareness of local varieties, enough to convince some supermarkets to begin carrying a greater range of apple varieties.

The economic prospects for a more diverse selection of apples appear better than they have been for more than a century. For one, the rapid growth of the cider, apple wine and apple brandy industries has made distinctive, bittersweet and bittersharp, tannin-rich apples desirable. With this new market, coupled with a growing interest in artisanal and place-based heritage foods, heirloom apple-growers have a strong base on which to bring back some of the tens of thousands of apple varieties that the global marketsplace has rendered endangered.

# Picking the Perfect Apple

> Why do we need so many different kinds of apples? Because
> there are so many different kinds of folks . . . There is merit in
> variety itself. It provides more points of contact with life, and
> leads away from uniformity and monotony.
>
> Liberty Hyde Bailey in *The Apple Tree* (1922)

Even for those who grew up far from the countryside, the
crisp autumn air and stunning shades of orange and red on
the trees seems to awaken some inherent urge to harvest. The
perennial lure of apple-picking does more than feed some
romantic seasonal longing, however – it also helps to sustain
small apple growers and to encourage the cultivation of a
wide range of apple types.

Unique apples are worth seeking out. Most supermarkets
carry only a handful of the thousands of distinct varieties of
apples that exist around the world. Roadside stands, farmers'
markets and orchards are some of the best places to find
fresh, locally grown apples. Even a locally grown MacIntosh
or Red Delicious, apples often found in supermarkets, can
taste remarkably different when eaten fresh from the tree.

Apples come in a staggering variety of colours, sizes,
shapes and flavours, some that many people may have never

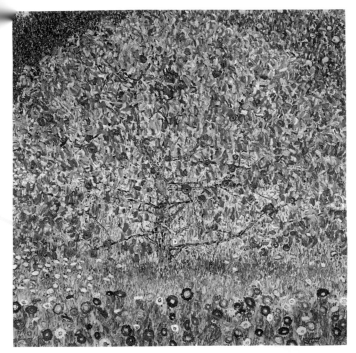

Gustav Klimt, *Apple Tree 1*, 1912.

experienced in an apple. The Roxbury Russet, for instance, has a rough brownish skin not unlike that of a potato. Many apples also have colourful names that hint at their particular time and place of origin: Wolf River, Cox's Orange Pippin, Gloria Mundi, Seek-No-Further, Belle de Boskoop, Fuji and Maid of Kent.

Apple-growers can provide guidance on finding apples at their peak, something that's not always easy to tell at a glance. Don't trust your eyes, because looks can be deceiving in the apple world. Some apples that appear humble, mottled and even misshapen can taste far better than their shiny, uniformly coloured cousins.

Picking the perfect apple involves a number of important factors. An apple's colour has always tempted eaters, a clever trick apples have used for centuries to entice animals and humans to indulge and, in the process, help to spread its seeds. Apples can range in colour from pale yellow to deep purply-red, with every imaginable combination of stripe, flush and freckle in between. North American varieties are some of the most vivid, in part because they were bred to have a dazzling palette. Early season apples usually reach full colour on the tree, while late keepers are often dull when picked and slowly develop their true colours in storage. The background or undercast colour of an apple often turns lighter as the apple ripens, while the surface colour tends to brighten or deepen.

An even, symmetrical fruit has long been highly regarded in the apple world. While today, even shapes help with packaging for shipping, in the past people demanded nicely shaped

Gustave Courbet, *Still-life with Apples*, 1871–2.

apples for their fine appearance on the dining table. Apple shapes can be roughly categorized as flat, round, conical and oblong, with many varieties falling in between. The Red Delicious, for example, is an oblong apple while the Golden Delicious varies from round-conical to oblong.

A large size is now considered essential to a good eating apple, but this wasn't always the case. Apple connoisseurs of the past believed that the best flavour could be found in medium-sized fruits, which were usually enjoyed as dessert. After eating many courses of meat and game, most people did not want anything more substantial (nor could any thing more fit in the stomach), and sharing a large piece of fruit was considered inappropriate. These inhibitions about large apples did not transfer to America, though, nor to Japan, where growers carefully breed apples weighing as much as 900 g (2 lb).

The texture of the skin and of the flesh of an apple is also important. Apple skins can be thick or thin, soft or tough. Victorians prized thin-skinned apples that seemed to melt in your mouth over the tough, waxy skins of apples like Baldwins. Some apples have skins that become greasy after picking, attracting dust that can dull the colour as well as be undesirable to touch. The texture of the flesh, too, can affect an apple's appeal. Although commercial growers favour crisp and juicy apples, apple varieties range from dry and crumbly to creamy and soft.

An apple's flavour depends on the balance of sweetness and acidity. Many commercial varieties are bred to taste very sweet at an early stage of maturity so they can be picked early, when the flesh is still firm enough to prevent bruising during transport. When flavours are balanced, the apple will be rich with plenty of sugar and acid for an intensely fruity taste. Too much acid makes apples sour, while too little makes apples bland. The tart apple Goldrush makes some people's mouths pucker even though it still has some sweetness. A Fuji apple, on the other hand, is mostly sweet and low in acid, even more so a month after its been picked. The best varieties of apples contain volatile compounds, such as ethers, aldehydes, esters and acetates, which are released as the apple is eaten. These compounds combine with the sugar and acid to give each variety its characteristic flavour. Nearly 200 different volatile compounds have been identified in Red and Golden Delicious apples alone.

Many factors influence an apple's flavour, size and appearance, but perhaps none so much as the weather. Many varieties need a warm summer and a long autumn to build up their sugars, aromas and depth of flavour; a cold, wet season is bad for many kinds of apples. Soil affects flavour, too, as does the age of the tree and where it is grown. The same variety can taste considerably different from region to region and from year to year. Flavours also seem to mirror the season in which the variety ripens. Summer apples tend to be light and crisp while later-maturing autumn and early winter apples are rich and complex, their skins often bronzed or russeted.

While all of these factors play an important role in determining an apple's appeal, the most important is ripeness. No matter how delicious an apple should be, one picked at the wrong time does not stand a chance. Apples picked too soon will be hard, acidic or starchy, while apples picked too late may be mushy and bland. Modern refrigeration and shipping has made some apple varieties available all of the time, making it easy to forget that fruit is seasonal and actually grown somewhere specific. All fruit has an optimal season when flavour and freshness are at their peak.

In the end, though, the perfect apple is a matter of personal preference. The following is a selection of apples that can sometimes be found at farmers' markets and orchards, with notes on their origins, uses and characteristics. The descriptions should only be taken as general guides, however. Like that of good wine, the quality of an apple depends on its growing conditions, handling and age.

**Ambri (India):** Native to Kashmir, the Ambri is a medium-sized apple, blushed red in colour with a crisp, sweet flesh that makes for excellent eating.

**Antonovka (Russia):** A hardy variety introduced in 1888 by Russian plant breeder Ivan Vladimirovich Michurin, this apple is large with green skin that ripens to yellow. Nicknamed the 'people's apple' for its popularity in eastern Europe and ability to sustain long harsh winters, the Antonovka is tart and especially well suited to making apple wine.

**Belle de Boskoop (France, Netherlands, Belgium):** Found in 1856 in Boskoop, Netherlands, this variety is medium to large in size and oval in shape, with a greenish-yellow colour under a dark red blush. Crisp, tart and aromatic, the flesh sweetens in storage. It holds its shape well in baking.

**Baldwin (United States):** Originating in Massachusetts around 1740, the Baldwin takes longer than most trees to bear its first fruit, about ten years. This large red apple is streaked with yellow and the flesh is firm and moderately tart; a good all-purpose apple.

**Ben Davis (United States):** Variously credited to nineteenth-century growers in Tennessee, Kentucky, Maine and Virginia, the Ben Davis is yellow with stripes, mottles and splashes of bright red. The yellowy flesh is aromatic and juicy but coarsely textured, working well in sauces.

**Cortland (United States):** A cross between a Ben Davis and a McIntosh, the Cortland was developed at the New York Agricultural Experiment Station and entered the commercial market in 1915. A red-and-green striped apple, the crisp, juicy flesh resists browning, making it excellent for salads and fruit cups.

**Cox's Orange Pippin (England):** Originating from a seed grown by Richard Cox at Slough, Buckinghamshire, England, around 1830, the Cox's Orange Pippin is sweet and aromatic with a yellow skin splashed with orange and red. The flesh is crisp, tender and juicy, making it an excellent dessert and cider apple.

**Empire (United States):** A cross between Red Delicious and McIntosh, the Empire came into commercial production by the New York Agricultural Experiment Station in 1966. Grown mostly in the Northeast and Midwest, the medium-sized apple is yellow and red (and sometimes all red). Its sweet and spicy flesh makes it excellent for eating out of hand.

**Esopus Spitzenburg (United States):** Known at least as far back as 1790 in Ulster County, New York, the Esopus Spitzenburg has a bright red blush over a yellow background with a hard, crisp, yellow flesh. Sweet and fruity, the apple is excellent in pies and is believed to be the inspiration for the Waldorf Salad. It's also said to have been the favourite eating apple of American president Thomas Jefferson.

**Fuji (Japan):** A cross made in Japan in 1939 between the American apples Rall's Genet and Red Delicious, this apple is yellow-green with an orange-red, sometimes pink, blush. The flesh is crisp and sweet and becomes sweeter with time.

**Ginger Gold (United States):** A chance seedling discovered in a Virginia orchard in the 1960s and originally named Harvey-licious, the Ginger Gold has a greenish-gold skin and a tart, crisp flavour with a sweet aftertaste, and is good for both eating and cooking.

**Gravenstein (Denmark, Germany):** Originating in Denmark or Germany, the Gravenstein is streaked with red and yellow over a greenish-yellow skin. Juicy and crisp, this variety has a reputation for being a very good cooking apple.

**Idared (United States):** Developed in Idaho from a cross of a Jonathan and a Wagener, the Idared is bright red with a creamy-white flesh that is sweetly tart. A good eating apple, its firmness also makes it good for baking. The flavour improves after several months of storage.

**Jonathan (United States):** Found on a farm in New York in 1826, the Jonathan was originally called Rick Apple. A medium-sized apple coloured red and yellow, the fruit is crisp and sweetly tart with a spicy aftertaste. Because it holds its shape so well, the Jonathan is frequently used for baking.

**Kinsei (Japan):** A cross of Golden Delicious and Ralls Janet, the Kinsei is a large yellow apple developed in Japan. Sweet and firm, the apple is good for cooking and eating.

**Lubsk Queen (Russia):** Introduced in Russia in 1880, the apple has a striking white skin with splashes of pink and red. The flesh is bright white and firm, with a brisk, tart flavour.

**Mutsu (Japan):** Developed in Japan, the Matsu, a descendent of the Golden Delicious, is a yellow-green apple with a coarser and juicier flesh than the Golden Delicious. It makes an excellent eating apple. It's sometimes called Crispin outside Japan.

**Northern Spy (United States):** A large sweet apple found in New York around 1800, the Northern Spy is yellow-green and heavily striped with red. Its mellow, creamy flesh is crisp and richly aromatic, great for pies as well as fresh eating.

**Rome Beauty (United States):** A chance seedling grown in Rome, Ohio, by Joel Gillett, the Rome Beauty is a deep red apple renowned for its beauty and reliability in the kitchen. When cooked, the apple retains its shape and the flesh acquires a rich flavour.

**Stayman (United States):** Raised in Kansas in 1866 from a Winesap seed, the Stayman is a medium-sized red or red striped over green apple with a violet cast. With a sweet-tart flavour and juicy flesh that holds its shape when cooked, this apple is a good all-purpose fruit.

A final word: be adventurous when selecting apples! Apples come in such a wide variety of flavours, some tasting of strawberries and others of nuts or honey, that even if you try one you don't like, you are sure to find some new favourites along the way.

# Recipes

Apples have pleased human palates for thousands of years, finding their way into the pots and onto the plates of cuisines around the world. The oldest apple core ever discovered was found in a Stone Age village in the Swiss Alps and is believed to be 300,000 years old. Nordic myths talk of gods eating golden apples to preserve their immortality. Persians munched on apples for dessert in the sixth century BCE. Roman gastronomer Apicius, who gave his name to the most complete cookbook to come down from antiquity, recorded a main dish recipe for apples cooked with pork and laced with coriander, liquamen (Roman fish sauce) and honey, though most Romans preferred their apples at the end of a meal to take advantage of their digestive and aphrodisiac properties.

Apples are combined with meat across northern and eastern Europe, South America, Turkey, Iran and Morocco. The acidity of the fruit helps to tenderize tougher cuts of meat. Combining apples with roasted pork is common almost everywhere except in Muslim countries where lamb is used instead. Moroccans often blend dried fruits or fresh apples into tagines of meat, vegetables and spices. Sausages are widely combined with apples in the American South, central Europe and Scandinavia.

The USA, France and England have nearly defined themselves by their apple desserts. The French prefer open-faced tarts while the English and Americans place chunks of apple in sturdy pie crusts. English dramatist and poet Robert Green wrote in 1590 that he could think of no greater compliment to give a beautiful woman than 'They breath is like the steame of apple-pyes.' Although the English can take credit for bringing apple pie to America, Americans have made the pie quintessentially their own, neatly summed up by the phrase 'as American as apple pie'. Early American pies were as robust as the colonists themselves, with the apples buried in hard, thick crusts that often played the part of both crust and cooking vessel. The first American cookbook, *American Cookery* by Amelia Simmons (1796), had two recipes for apple pie and one for Marlborough pudding, a pie calling for stewed apples rather than fresh apple slices. Fritters, dumplings, crisps, pancakes, grunts, cobblers, pandowdys and slumps are other versions of baked, spiced apples popular in North America, Britain and parts of Europe.

Apples are also popular in Mexico and Central America, prominent at markets, fairs and even religious rituals in the late summer and early autumn. Apples are eaten fresh, sliced up in salads and preserved as jellies, jams and fruit liqueurs. In some parts of Mexico, apples are combined with carrots to make a thick drink. Apples are also sautéed with eggs for breakfast.

Cider has also found its way into food, and is used as a base for stews, soups and braises of meats, vegetables and beans. Hundreds of cider dishes are common to Spain, France, Quebec, New England and the American South.

## Ensalada de Remolacha con Manzana Verde (Argentinian Beetroot and Green Apple Salad)

Apples are a common ingredient in South American salads.

3–4 medium-sized beetroot (beets)
1 Granny Smith apple
½ cup (8 tablespoons) olive oil
1 lemon
salt

Peel and boil the beetroot until soft enough to pierce with a fork. Cut into bite-sized (about ½ inch/2 cm) pieces. Core the apple and cut into bite-sized pieces. Combine the apples and beetroot in a bowl. Drizzle with olive oil and squeeze with lemon juice. Stir to combine. Can be served cold or at room temperature.

## Apple, Asian Pear and Walnut Haroseth

Haroseth, a mixture of fruit, nuts and honey, is one of the six elements of the seder plate, and symbolizes the mortar used by Israelite slaves in Egypt. Recipes for haroseth can vary greatly depending on the country, though apples are a common ingredient. Used as a condiment, haroseth is good with many kinds of roasted meat.

1 ¼ cups (225 g) walnut halves
1 Granny Smith apple, peeled, cored, cut into ⅓-inch (6 mm) cubes
1 Asian pear, peeled, cored, cut into ⅓-inch (6 mm) cubes
3 tablespoons sweet Passover wine (substitute apple, orange or grape juice)
2 tablespoons honey
1 teaspoon finely grated orange zest
¾ teaspoon ground cinnamon
chopped fresh mint

Chop nuts and place in medium bowl. Add apple, pear, wine, honey, orange zest and cinnamon. Stir to blend, adding more honey, if desired.

## Apple Moyse

Apple moyse is an old English dessert for which no two recipes seem to agree. It's essentially a Tudor apple sauce.

1 ½ lbs (700 g) apples
1 cup (240 ml) water

2 egg yolks
2 tablespoons sugar
2 tablespoons butter
pinch of ginger and cinnamon

Peal, core and cut the apples into ½-inch (2-cm) thick slices. Stew over medium heat in a heavy covered saucepan with water until soft. Puree apples in blender or by rubbing through a sieve. Return puree to saucepan, stir in egg yolks, sugar and butter, stirring continuously until boiling. Pour puree into dish and allow to cool before serving. Sprinkle with ginger and cinnamon.

## Fricassée à la Matius
## (Pork Stew with Apples)

The oldest known apple recipe comes from *De Re Coquinaria* (The Art of Cooking), a collection of recipes attributed to Apicius, the famed Roman epicure who lived in the first century CE. The recipe was named for Matius, a friend of Caesar, who wrote a book on domestic science. The apples called for in the dish are also named for him.

Put in a saucepan pan oil, liquamen and stock. Chop up leek, coriander and small meatballs. Dice cooked pork shoulder with the crackling left on. Cook all together. Half way through the cooking, add Matian apples, cored and diced. While this is cooking, grind together pepper, mint, cumin, fresh coriander or coriander seed, mint and asafetida root. Pour in vinegar, honey, liquamen, a little grape must and some of the cooking broth. Mix with a little vinegar. Bring to the boil. When it has boiled, crumble bits of pastry to thicken the sauce. Sprinkle with pepper and serve.

# Wassail

Bless the apple trees for the coming of spring and ward off evil with this traditional beverage. The name is derived from the Old Norse 'Ves heill', which translates as 'good health'. Recipes for wassail vary widely, and can be based on beer, wine or cider. This recipe is based on a Tudor concoction.

10 small apples
10 teaspoons brown sugar
2 bottles dry sherry or dry Madeira
½ teaspoon grated nutmeg
1 teaspoon ground ginger
3 cloves
3 allspice berries
1 stick cinnamon
2 cups (200 g) icing (superfine) sugar
½ cup (120 ml) water
6 eggs, separated
1 cup (240 ml) brandy

Heat oven to 175°C/350°F. Core the apples and fill each with a tea-spoon of brown sugar. Place in a baking pan and fill the bottom with ⅛ inch (3 mm) of water. Bake for 30 minutes or until tender. Set aside.

Combine the sherry or Madeira, nutmeg, ginger, cloves, allspice berries, cinnamon, sugar and water in a large, heavy saucepan and heat without letting the mixture come to the boil. Leave on very low heat.

Meanwhile, beat the egg yolks until light and lemon-coloured. Beat the whites until stiff and fold them into the yolks. Strain the wine mixture and add gradually to the eggs, stirring constantly. Add the brandy. Pour into a metal punch bowl and float the apples on top.

Serves 10

# Waldorf Salad

Invented in 1896 by the maître d'hôtel Oscar Tschirky at the Waldorf-Astoria Hotel in New York, this simple apple salad was an instant success. The original recipe, below, in Tschirky's 1896 cookbook called only for apples, celery and mayonnaise – none of the grapes and nuts that often get added today.

3 apples chopped into ½-inch (2-cm) pieces
⅔ cup (100 g) chopped celery
⅓ cup (80 ml) mayonnaise

Combine apples and celery in a medium-sized bowl. Pour in mayonnaise and toss until completely coated. Serve immediately or chill overnight.

# Braised Red Cabbage, Apples and Sausage

Apples and sausage are in no short supply in Germany, where they are often served with cabbage.

4 tablespoons rendered bacon fat
2 tablespoons sugar
1 small yellow onion, chopped
4 cups (600 g) shredded red cabbage
2 tart red apples, such as Jonathan, cored and sliced thin
but not peeled
2 tablespoons cider vinegar
½ teaspoon caraway seeds
1–1½ lb (450–700 g) German or Polish style smoked
sausage links, or bratwursts
1 lb (450 g) new potatoes
salt and fresh ground black pepper to taste
1 cup (240 ml) beer

Melt the bacon fat in a large frying pan over medium heat. Add the sugar and cook, stirring often, until the sugar browns, about 4 minutes. Reduce the heat to medium low, add the onion and sauté until it is golden, about 5 minutes. Add the cabbage, apples, vinegar and caraway seeds, and stir to blend.

Place the sausage links and the potatoes on top of the cabbage mixture, and season with salt and pepper. Pour the beer over the sausage, potatoes and cabbage. Bring the mixture to the boil over a medium high heat. Once boiling, reduce the heat and simmer, covered, for 45 minutes. Add salt and pepper as needed. Serve hot.

## *Huevos zacatlantecos*
## (Mexican sautéed apples and eggs)

A popular apple fair held in early August in Zacatlan, Puebla, Mexico, celebrates the start of the apple season in the region. This is a popular breakfast dish that time of year in this apple-centric region of the country.

6 eggs
2 tablespoons finely chopped parsley
pinch of salt and pepper
4 tablespoons butter
1 large apple, unpeeled, cored and sliced into crescents

Beat the eggs with parsley, salt, and pepper. In a frying pan, melt the butter and sautee the apples until crisp tender. Pour in the egg mixture. Turn the pan as the eggs set around the edges. When the bottom is set, turn the eggs carefully to cook the other side. Alternatively, place in the oven and grill until lightly browned. Cut into wedges and serve immediately.
Serves 4

# Apple Pie

More than 36 million Americans claim apple as their favourite pie filling, though there may also be 36 million versions of the pie. This is the version my childhood babysitter used to make, the first apple pie I'd ever eaten.

*Crust (for a two-crusted pie)*
2 cups (240 g) flour
1 ½ teaspoons salt
⅓ cup (80 ml) ice water
¾ cup (140 g) shortening (fat)
¼ cup (60 g) butter

*Filling*
12 apples, peeled, cored and diced
⅓ cup (65 g) white sugar
½ teaspoon cinnamon
⅛ teaspoon nutmeg
⅛ teaspoon ground cloves
1 tablespoon fresh lemon juice
6 tablespoons melted butter
⅓ cup (65 g) brown sugar
1 heaped tablespoon cornstarch/cornflour

Preheat oven to 190°C/375°F.
Blend flour and salt. Cut fat into flour with a pastry knife until it resembles coarse meal with pea-sized pieces. Mix in water with a fork using only as much as needed for dough to form a ball. Roll out dough and chill for two hours or up to overnight.

Combine apples with sugar, cinnamon, nutmeg, cloves, lemon juice and butter in a mixing bowl. Pour mixture into a covered baking dish and bake for 40 minutes. Remove from oven. Drain juice from baked apples into small saucepan and set the apple mixture aside. Mix brown sugar and cornstarch into the juice of the baked apples. Stir over high heat until boiling. Remove from heat and pour sauce over apples and stir.

Raise oven temperature to 230°C/450°F.

Remove dough from refrigerator and divide into two equal parts. Gently shape into two flat, round discs. Line pie plate with one of the rounds.

Pour apple mixture in pastry-lined pie dish. Cover with top crust, crimp and prick holes or make vents. Bake at 230°C/450°F for 15 minutes, then at 170°C/350°F for 35 minutes or until crust is golden brown. Leave to cool and serve.


## Braised Chorizos

Cider has been made in Spain for hundreds of years. This recipe combines cider with the traditional spiced Spanish sausage, chorizo.

6 2-oz (55-g) semi-dry Spanish chorizos
2 tablespoons olive oil
24 fl. oz (700 ml) hard cider

Cut four ½ inch deep slashes into one side of each sausage. In a medium frying pan, heat olive oil. Add chorizos and cook over moderate heat, turning occasionally, until lightly browned, about 5 minutes.

Add the cider and bring to a boil over high heat. Reduce heat to medium and cook until chorizos are soft and the liquid is reduced to about 2/3 cup (160 ml), about 30 minutes. Transfer to a shallow bowl and serve with hunks of bread.


## *Apfelstrudel* (apple strudel)

A traditional Austrian and German pastry, so popular that there's even an 'apple strudel show' in the Court Bakery at Schoenbrunn Palace in Vienna. While strudels can have many different fillings, apple is the most well known and popular. This recipe is adapted from Rick Rogers' *Kaffeehaus: Exquisite Desserts from the Classic Cafes of Vienna, Budapest, and Prague.*

*Filling*
2 tablespoons golden rum
3 tablespoons raisins
¼ teaspoon ground cinnamon
⅓ cup plus 1 tablespoon (70 g) sugar
½ cup (120 g) unsalted butter, melted, divided
1½ cups (90 g) fresh breadcrumbs
½ cup (75 g) coarsely chopped walnuts
2 lb (900 g) tart cooking apples, peeled, cored and cut into
¼-inch-thick (5-mm-thick) slices

Preheat the oven to 200°C/400°F/gas mark 6. Line a baking sheet with parchment paper.

Mix the rum and raisins in a bowl. Mix the cinnamon and sugar in another bowl. Heat 3 tablespoons of butter in a large frying pan over medium-high heat. Add the breadcrumbs and cook, stirring often, until golden, about 3 minutes. Let cool.

*Dough*
1⅓ cups (160 g) unbleached flour
⅛ teaspoon salt
7 tablespoons water,
plus more if needed
2 tablespoons vegetable oil, plus additional for
coating the dough
½ teaspoon cider vinegar

Combine flour and salt in a food-mixer fitted with the paddle attachment. Mix the water, oil and vinegar in a separate bowl. Add the water-oil-vinegar mixture to the flour with the mixer on a low speed until a soft dough forms. Add more water if too dry.

Change to the dough hook and knead dough on medium until it forms a ball with a rough surface. Remove dough from the mixer and continue kneading by hand on an unfloured surface for about 2 minutes. Shape the dough into a ball and transfer to a plate. Oil the top of the dough lightly. Cover the ball tightly with plastic wrap and allow to stand for 30 to 90 minutes (longer is better).

Cover working area (you'll need a space roughly 2 x 3 feet, or 60 x 90 cm) with a table cloth. Dust with flour and rub into the fabric. Uncover dough and place in the middle of the cloth. Roll the dough as thin as you can over the cloth. Pick up the dough by one edge and begin to gently stretch and pull the dough, being careful not to tear it. Stretch and pull the dough with the back of your hand until it is about 2 feet wide by 3 feet long (60 x 90 cm). The dough will be tissue-thin. Cut away any excess dough with scissors. The dough is now ready to be filled.

Using dough on tablecloth, spread 3 tablespoons of remaining melted butter over dough with your hands, being careful not to tear the dough. Sprinkle the buttered breadcrumbs over the dough. Spread the walnuts about 3 inches (7.5 cm) from the short edge of the dough in a 6-inch-wide (15 cm-wide) strip. Mix the apples with the raisin-rum mixture. Add the cinnamon and sugar. Spread the mixture over the walnuts.

Fold the short end of the dough over the filling. Lift the tablecloth at the short end of the dough so the strudel rolls onto itself. Transfer strudel to the prepared baking sheet. Curve the dough into a U-shape to fit. Tuck the ends under the strudel and brush the top with the remaining melted butter.

Bake the strudel for 30 minutes or until it is a deep golden brown. Cool for at least 30 minutes before slicing.

## Tarte Tatin

A famous French upside-down apple tart thought to have originated in 1888 when Stephanie Tatin, co-owner with her sister of l'Hotel Tatin in Lamotte-Beuvron, France, accidentally assembled her apple tart in backwards order. She served the tart anyway and it soon became a trademark dessert of the hotel.

¼ cup (60 g) (half a stick) of unsalted butter
⅔ cup (130 g) sugar
8 firm apples
1 sheet frozen puff pastry

Preheat oven to 190°C/375°F.

Peel, core and quarter the apples. Over a low heat in a heavy, ovenproof 10–12-inch (25–30 cm) frying pan, melt the butter. Add the sugar and stir occasionally until it reaches a golden caramel colour, about 5 minutes.

Arrange apple quarters in pan, working your way from the outside in, overlapping slices to create a circular pattern until the pan is covered. Place lid on top and cook slowly over medium heat for 15–20 minutes until the apples are juicy and tender and the juice is reduced to a thick caramel.

Roll out pastry sheet to ½ inch (1 cm) thick and cut into a circle slightly larger than your pan. Tuck edge of pastry down into the pan, covering the apples completely. Bake until the crust is golden-brown, about 25–30 minutes.

Remove from the oven and allow to cool on a rack for about 30 minutes.

Run a sharp knife along the inside edges of the pan. Place a plate or other serving dish on top of the pan and quickly flip the pan. Gently lift the pan from the plate as the apples drop down over the puffed pastry. Serve warm.

# Select Bibliography

Barboza, David, 'Export Apple of China's Eye Is, er, Apples',
    *New York Times* (2 April 2003)

Bailey, Liberty Hyde, ed., *The Standard Cyclopedia of Horticulture:*
    *A Discussion for the Amateur, and the Professional and Commercial*
    *Grower, of the Kinds, Characteristics and Methods of Cultivation of*
    *the Species of Plants Grown in the Regions of the United States and*
    *Canada for Ornament, for Fancy, for Fruit and for Vegetables; with*
    *Keys to the Natural Families and Genera, Descriptions of the*
    *Horticultural Capabilities of the States and Provinces and*
    *Dependent Islands, and Sketches of Eminent Horticulturists*
    (New York, 1915)

Browning, Frank, *Apples* (New York, 1998)

Correnty, Paul, *The Art of Cidermaking* (Boulder, CO, 1995)

Davidson, Hilda, *Myths and Symbols in Pagan Europe: Early*
    *Scandinavian and Celtic Religions* (Syracuse, NY, 1988)

Delumeau, Jean, *History of Paradise: The Garden of Eden in Myth*
    *and Tradition*, trans. Matthew O'Connell (London, 1995)

Deng, Xiuxin, 'Fruit Production and Export of China', United
    Nations Asian and Pacific Centre for Agricultural
    Engineering and Machinery (Beijing, 2006)

Edge, John T., *Apple Pie: An American Story* (New York, 2004)

Hedrick, U. P., *A History of Horticulture in America* (Portland, OR,
    1988)

Heng, Zhai, Guo Ling, Yao Yuxin and Shu Huairui, 'Review of
    the Chinese Apple Industry', *Acta Horticulturae*, DCCLXXII,

International Horticulture Congress

Janson, H. Frederic, *Pomona's Harvest: An Illustrated Chronicle of Antiquarian Fruit Literature* (Portland, OR, 1996)

Juniper, Barrie Edward, *The Story of the Apple* (Portland, OR, 2006)

Kim, Jihyun, 'South Korea Apple Case: The Impact of WTO's Trade Liberalization on South Korea's Apple Market', *TED Case Studies*, no. 670 (2003)

Lynd, Mitch, 'Great Moments in Apple History', Midwest Apple Improvement Association, at www.hort.purdue.edu/newcrop/maia/history.html (accessed September 2010)

Macoun, W. T., 'Apple Breeding in Canada', *Journal of Heredity*, 8 (1912), pp. 479–87

Martin, Alice A., *All About Apples* (New York, 1976)

Mitham, Peter J., 'Fruit "for the Cold North": Canada's Russian Apple Trials, 1888–1908', in *Canadian Environments: Essays in Culture, Politics and History*, ed. Robert C. Thomsen and Nannette Hale (Montreal, 2005)

Moore, James N., *Fruit Breeding* (New York, 1996)

Morgan, Joan, and Alison Richards, *The Book of Apples* (London, 1993)

O'Rourke, Andrew Desmond, ed., *Understanding the Japanese Food and Agrimarket: A Multifaceted Opportunity* (Binghamton, NY, 1994)

Oraguzie, N. C., J. Soejima, T. Fukusawa-Akada, K. Kudo, H. Komatsu and N. Kotoda, 'Apple Breeding Progress in Japan', *Acta Horticulturae* (ISHS), DCXXII, pp. 583–90, at www.actahort.org/books/622/622_62.htm (accessed September 2010)

Orton, Vrest, *The American Cider Book* (New York, 1995)

Patent, Greg, *A is for Apple: More than 200 Recipes for Eating, Munching, and Cooking with America's Favorite Fruit* (New York, 1999)

Pirog, Rich, and John Tyndall, 'Comparing Apples to Apples: An Iowa perspective on Apples and Local Food Systems', *Apple Journal*, at www.applejournal.com/art001a.htm (accessed April 2010)

Pollan, Michael, 'Breaking Ground: The Call of the Wild Apple', *New York Times* (5 November 1998)

—, *The Botany of Desire: A Plant's-Eye View of the World* (New York, 2001)

Price, Robert, *Johnny Appleseed, Man and Myth* (Gloucester, MA, 1967)

Proux, Annie, and Lew Nichols, *Cider: Making, Using and Enjoying Sweet and Hard Cider* (North Adams, MA, 2003)

Thoreau, Henry David, 'Wild Apples', in *The Natural History Essays*, intro. and notes by Robert Satelmeyer (Salt Lake City, UT, 1980)

Minnesota Landscape Arboretum, 'Fruit Breeding', University of Minnesota, at www.arboretum.umn.edu/fruitbreeding.aspx (accessed September 2010)

Watson, Ben, *Cider, Hard and Sweet: History, Traditions and Making Your Own*, 2nd edn (Woodstock, VT, 2008)

Weber, Bruce, *The Apple in America: The Apple in 19th Century American Art* (New York, 1993)

Williams, R. R., *Cider and Juice Apples* (Bristol, 1988)

Wynne, Peter, *Apples: History, Folklore, Horticulture and Gastronomy* (New York, 1975)

Yepson, Roger, *Apples* (New York, 1994)

Zai-Long, Li, 'Deciduous Fruit Production in China', FAO: Regional Office for Asia and the Pacific (March 1999)

# Websites and Associations

All About Apples
www.allaboutapples.com

American Pomological Society
americanpomological.org

Apple Journal
www.applejournal.com

The Big Apple Association
www.bigapple.org.uk

Botanical: A Modern Herbal
botanical.com

Cornell Orchards, Cornell University, Ithaca, NY, USA
hort.cals.cornell.edu/cals/hort/about/cornell_orchards.cfm

East Malling Research Station, Kent, UK
www.emr.ac.uk

Fruit Growers News (fruit industry publication)
fruitgrowersnews.com

Japan: National Agriculture and Food Research Organization
www.naro.affrc.go.jp

Orange Pippin: The Comprehensive Resource for Apples and Orchards
www.orangepippin.com

Seed Savers Historic Orchard, Decorah, Iowa, USA
www.seedsavers.org

United States Apple Association
www.usapple.org

Washington State Apple Association
www.bestapples.com

What's Cooking America: History and Legends of Apples
whatscookingamerica.net/Fruit/Apples.htm

# Acknowledgements

It's amazing how quickly a subject can permeate your life, not to mention the lives of those around you if you are anything like me and are unable to keep anything of what you've learned to yourself. So thanks to my many friends and coworkers, and my parents, for listening and at least pretending to be interested in what I had to say. Those who dared to go apple-picking with me in this time period, Natasha, Nicole and Charlie, deserve particular thanks.

Thanks to Andrew F. Smith and Reaktion Books for the opportunity to contribute to the Edible series. Thanks also to Seed Savers for a delightful afternoon in the heritage apple orchard and to the countless growers I pelted with questions at local farmers markets. Any error in the book is mine, and any success thanks to all those who have ever written, grown or had anything to say about apples.

Finally, thanks to Matt, who lived with this book, too, and willingly drove hours to eat apples far past their prime without complaint. I would be lost without his support and encouragement.

# Photo Acknowledgements

The author and the publishers wish to thanks to the below sources of illustrative material and/or permission to reproduce it.

Author's collection: pp. 86, 87; Bodleian Library, University of Oxford: pp. 22, 48; © The Trustees of the British Museum, London: pp. 20, 29, 34, 36, 43, 59, 60; The Cleveland Museum of Art, Cleveland, Ohio, USA: pp. 12 (Bequest of Leonard C. Hanna, Jr. 1958.47), 51 (Bequest of Ralph King. 1926.485); The John C. and Susan L. Huntingdon Archive of Buddhist and Related Art, Cleveland, Ohio, USA: p. 84; Istockphoto: p. 6 (Gustavo Andrade); Matthew Jensen, 2009: pp. 95, 97, 98; Library of Congress, Washington DC, USA: pp. 26, 61, 64, 66, 74, 78; Musée d'Orsay: p. 93; Illuminated Manuscript Collection, Princeton University, USA: p. 31; Stock Xchng: pp. 11 (Patrick Hajzler), 62 (Naneki), 79 (Rogojel), 82 (Amy J. Pollock), 89 (Rachel Kirk), 90 (Brandon W. Mosley), 92 (Robert Mitchie), 94 (Rai Varpunen); S. M. Amin/Saudi Aramco World/SAWDIA: p. 37; William Tracy/Saudi Aramco World/SAWDIA: p.16; Terra Foundation for American Art, Chicago, Illinois, USA: p.53; University of California, San Diego, USA: pp. 8, 45, 49; University of North Dakota Cass County Extension: p. 14; US Library of Medicine, Bethesda, MD, USA: p. 75; The Victoria and Albert Museum, London: pp. 16, 32, 57, 72; Werner Forman Archive: pp. 35 (Courtesy of Bruce McAlpine, London), 40 (Palazzo dei Conservatori, Rome).

# Index

*italic* numbers refer to illustrations; **bold** to recipes